LIKE PUNK NEVER HAPPENED

Like Punk Never Happened

Culture Club and the New Pop

DAVE RIMMER

faber and faber

This edition first published in 2011
by Faber and Faber Ltd
Bloomsbury House, 74–77 Great Russell Street
London WC1B 3DA

A CIP record for this book is available from the British Library

ISBN 978–0–571–28026–1

*For my mother, for the gift of language which was
stolen from her.
For my father, because I forgot his birthday again.
And for Laurence Sheppard, wherever the hell he is.*

PLATES

Preface to the 2011 Edition

Some time in 1984, as the New Pop – to use this particular book's terminology – began to enter its 'imperial' phase, it was becoming clear that the editorial team which had ushered *Smash Hits* magazine through its early-1980s golden age was soon going to break up. Editor Mark Ellen was about to follow his predecessor Dave Hepworth upstairs at publisher Emap, where the pair would launch *Q* and later *Mojo* before going independent with *Word*. Features editor Ian Birch was moving to *Just Seventeen*, the next step on what was to become a stellar career in transatlantic magazine publishing. Designer Steve Bush would take over as *Smash Hits* editor for a while before heading off to create his own publishing empire in Australia. And Neil Tennant was poised to try his luck as a Pet Shop Boy, with what would prove to be the most conspicuous success of all. My ambition was a little more modest. I just wanted to publish a first book before I turned 30.

I'd started writing for *Smash Hits* in 1981, my first, stuttering year as a young print media freelance. A spell as one of the assistant editors at *Time Out* magazine was ended by a staff strike in spring of that year. A new London music weekly called *Trax* had run my first few attempts at music journalism, but then publisher Girl About Town pulled the plug. By early summer I was short of work, but had acquired a sprinkling of contacts around London as staff from those two publications moved into positions elsewhere.

One such was Mark Ellen, who'd liked my stuff when features editor at *Trax*, and was now in a similar job at *Smash Hits*. Editor Dave Hepworth, also new in his role, initially wasn't so keen, but Mark smuggled me in while Dave was on holiday. Soon I was a regular contributor, running around to interview the emerging pop stars of the day. Weirdly, by an entirely different route, Neil Tennant also began writing for *Smash Hits* at exactly the same time. Neil and I had been friendly through our teens in Newcastle – both members of the Saturday morning Young People's Theatre and the same glam-era party circuit – and were pleasantly surprised to encounter each other again. In a further twist of synchronicity (a term popularized in that period by yet another Geordie, Sting) the photographer (later filmmaker) Eric Watson, who had roots in the same crowd, also began contributing to *Smash Hits* right then. People sometimes referred to the three of us as the magazine's 'Newcastle mafia'.

Smash Hits was by no means the only publication I worked for in the early 1980s. At a time when everything was still done on manual typewriters and finished copy was delivered to editors by hand, I'd take a bus to the West End and scatter my copy around the print media of the day. Among commissions for assorted Sunday supplements and women's magazines, I regularly contributed to Nick Logan's independent monthly *The Face* (which was like *Smash Hits'* older cousin) and combined writing with informal editorial roles at *City Limits* (a London listings magazine born out of the *Time Out* strike), *Kicks* (a left-leaning independent teenage monthly), and *New Sounds New Styles* (a New Romantic-focused *Smash Hits* spin-off designed by Malcolm Garrett). But as I moved up the feature writers' pecking order and began to get involved in the production of the magazine, it was *Smash Hits* that came to seem like home.

Apart from anything else, it was just so much more fun than all the other mags. The office was in Carnaby Street, at that time a sort of elephant's graveyard of street culture, directly over the road from our inky rivals at the *NME* and one floor lower. You'd sometimes notice their journalists peering down into what we were pleased to learn they called our 'Smash Hits playpen', gloomily wondering how this impertinent young rag had come to be more hip than they were and acquired a vastly bigger circulation in the process. Their editorial team was fractious and faction-ridden, ours was tight and friendly. The entire editorial and art staff – nine or ten of us – fitted into one room small enough for everyone to talk to each other without leaving their desks, even if you had to shout over the clatter of typewriters and whatever was on the office record player. (Neil and I were in the best position to control this instrument, which meant a lot of dance and disco.)

The working day would begin with one big conversation, as people reported back on gigs seen the night before, clubs and parties dutifully attended, albums heard, stuff seen on television, and pop stars interviewed. These informal discussions, which often resumed over lunch at the Bonbonniere on the corner of Great Marlborough Street, were as reflective as they were anecdotal, and *Like Punk Never Happened* owes a debt to them both for some of its tone and plenty of its perspectives.

This was a bright and talented crowd, as well as an extremely funny one. As we banged out the bits and pieces of the magazine, or chipped in to the communal headline-writing sessions, laughter would bounce around the office all day – sometimes I'd duck into the foyer to calm down, but even the receptionist, Samantha Archer, was hilarious – and the jokes would land on the page. One of these was the phrase 'like punk never happened', coined by Neil after Paul Weller had said something to that effect in an interview while describing the VIP behaviour of Spandau Ballet. The phrase was then applied gleefully, with varying degrees of irony, to any image of pop excess. It stuck around in the *Smash Hits* lexicon for a long time, although we'd regularly overhaul the 'bollocks', as we called our repertoire of stock jokes and phrases, to stop things getting stale. 'What's new bollocks for the word "fab"?' I remember once shouting in frustration from my typewriter.

Some of the things I learnt in those *Smash Hits* production periods have stayed with me ever since: the value of mischief, the beauty of concision, the importance of having fun with your work and how to use that in giving personality to a publication, the necessity of never underestimating your audience.

Smash Hits' fortnightly schedule for me meant one week of production, one week of doing interviews and writing. In the beginning this usually meant meeting young hopefuls ('We're looking for a fresh new sound') in the record company offices which in those days were still mostly clustered in Soho. Soon I graduated to bigger stars in more interesting circumstances. As Kurt Vonnegut's Bokonon put it, unexpected travel plans are dancing lessons from God, and I grabbed at every opportunity for a trip. Not only were they one of the major perks of a rather poorly paid profession (a replacement suitcase I once had to purchase in Osaka wiped out a quarter of my fee for a two-week job), but they were also the best way to get to know the people you were writing about. In the record company offices, you were usually just one of a procession of journalists on interview day – part of the 'them' to their 'us'. But all that changed in Los Angeles or Munich, where suddenly you became a piece of home, sharing their outsider perspective and laughing along at weird interview questions and indigenous fan behaviour.

As the 1980s got into gear the rise of *Smash Hits* paralleled the increasingly international success of British pop groups – notably Spandau Ballet, Duran Duran, Culture Club and Wham! Both their careers and our circulation depended on lots of coverage, and the magazine developed an almost symbiotic relationship with these groups. If you got on well with a band, you tended to be assigned to them on a regular basis. In 1983–84 I was both the Duran Duran correspondent and the Culture Club correspondent, lucky enough to catch the last great days of music industry largesse, travelling with these two very different groups to Paris, New York, Tokyo, Sydney. Not only did you acquire an insider's view of the pop process on these trips, you also ended up hanging around with all the session musicians, management personnel and record company types who were also along for the ride. There was no better way to find out everything that was going on. My problem was never what to put into a story, only what was best to leave out.

Neil Tennant had a background in book publishing – before coming to *Smash Hits* he had been an editor at two illustrated book publishers – and he and I were always talking about book ideas. Sometime in early summer 1984 we decided it would be a good idea for me to write a book about what was now, clearly, the most successful period of British pop music since the mid-1960s. For me, knowing that as the editorial team broke up I would soon be moving on to something else, it seemed a good way to draw a line under the whole experience, make some sense of it, get a book into print. Neil would function as my agent and editor. In the champagne bar at Kettner's, a popular media haunt in those pre-Groucho Club days, we spent an evening making notes about the topics this book should cover. The idea was always to combine a general overview with the story of a particular group, and Culture Club, then at the very peak of their popularity, seemed the best bet. I knocked up a proposal for a book which at that point was called simply 'Pop Music', and discussed it with Jon Moss in Tokyo, but it was impossible to get any commitment from the group. ('We're a bit concerned', Roy Hay would tell me, 'about the chapter called "Sex".') The way it worked out (described in chapter 11) left me feeling a little dissed, and some of my annoyance certainly crept into the text.

Neil, meanwhile, started hawking the proposal to publishers. He didn't have to look too far. Faber, with Pete Townshend recently installed as acquiring editor, were looking to establish a pop culture list, and were immediately keen. Neil and I had various congenial but slightly perplexing meetings with Townshend, who always did most of the talking, and soon, along with Jon Savage's Kinks biography and Paul Morley's interview collection, *Ask*, 'Pop Music' was formally commissioned to launch the list. I was thrilled to be at Faber, home of so many literary stars. (Malcolm Garrett would later design the book to a brief of making it look like the typographic Faber covers I remembered from my youth.) Faber in turn were intrigued to observe the ways of the music journalist. Jon Savage and I were friends, but neither of us got on with Paul Morley. At one Faber party, Jon had a huge, public row with Morley. At another Faber party, Neil and I had a similar contretemps with both Morley and his fellow *NME* journalist Ian Penman, during which Neil got so cross that he kicked Morley in the shin. Shortly after that, Faber managing director Matthew Evans tapped Jon on the shoulder one day. 'You lot,' he said. 'You're worse than the poets!'

At the beginning of 1985 I sat down to work on the book. I'd basically given myself a dozen essay titles, and now had just three months to figure them all out. In the end it took four. I can't remember exactly when the title changed, but one day it struck me: *Like Punk Never Happened*. Not only did it have more of a twinkle than the drily definitive 'Pop Music', it also crystallized one of the book's essential arguments – that, although the gaudy trappings of New Pop stardom made it look indeed 'like punk never happened', if punk hadn't first prised open the business of music then all the Durans and Boy Georges would never have happened either.

The first few chapters were written in the Islington flat of Culture Club backing singer, Helen Terry. She and I had become friendly in Japan, and I was cat-sitting while she was in Detroit recording with Don Was. When those sessions were abruptly curtailed I moved my typewriter to the old Kicks office at the Diorama in Regent's Park. Neighbouring offices were inhabited by David Toop and *Collusion* magazine, Martin Goldschmidt of Cooking Vinyl, and R. D. Laing's charity the Philadelphia Association. Not that I was in much of a state to talk to anyone. The first chapter took a month to complete, the whole second half of the book was written in three weeks flat, and the introduction was banged out in about 45 minutes, Neil anxious at my shoulder, before a final mad dash to Faber. The paragraphs about Live Aid in the Postscript were added months later, at the proofing stage.

In retrospect, Live Aid marked the point where it all went wrong. Wham! went their separate ways, Spandau Ballet were down the dumper, Duran Duran fragmented into Arcadia and the Power Station, never to regain their momentum, and Culture Club split up while Boy George went off on his heroin-fuelled lost weekend with Marilyn.

At the time it seemed colossal bad luck. The subject of my book had fallen on his sword before the thing had even arrived in the shops. But then so had the whole New Pop. The crucial characteristic of *Like Punk Never Happened* is that it was, quite self-consciously, written entirely from inside the phenomenon it describes – and I caught pretty much the last point at which it was possible to do that.

While I was writing, Neil, who talked the chapters over with me as I embarked on them, and gave the finished ones an edit, was mostly busy at Advision studios in the West End, where various T. Rex hits had been recorded. I did a lot of work listening to the 12-track demo that had won Pet Shop Boys their deal with EMI, and one day Neil arrived with the new version of 'West End Girls', freshly transcribed to cassette. I must have been the first person outside the studio to hear a recording that would soon be number one in 15 countries. This would make meetings with Faber a bit irritating – they now all seemed more interested in the career of my pop star agent than in discussing my damned book – but in retrospect it was a landmark too. The 'pervy synth-pop duo' might survive, but pop had shifted in a new, dance-orientated direction. Within a few years, outrageously clad pop stars had been replaced in the charts by faceless house producers and manufactured boy bands. Staples of the *Like Punk Never Happened* era, such as the BBC chart show *Top of the Pops* and eventually *Smash Hits* too, would fall by the wayside, at least in part because of pop's new lack of personality.

Everyone around Culture Club seemed to really like the book, but the band themselves weren't too happy. None of them had spoken to me since I announced I was writing it, but Jon Moss was straight on the phone the morning John Blake in the *Mirror*, having got hold of an advance copy, splashed the 'amazing story' that Jon and George were lovers. It was a ludicrously open secret, but after due deliberation – it was impossible to understand the band without the fact, which also cut right to the confluence of sex and ambition which has long lain at the heart of pop success – I had become the first to spell it out. I'd done so as tactfully as I could – underplayed it, really – but Jon was furious and called me a cunt in *i-D* magazine. We'd always been quite friendly – sufficiently so that George had become convinced I was trying to steal his man – and later were able to make our peace.

George was angry too, of course, and sounded off about me here and there. Unless I had 'employed Sherlock Holmes,' he told the *Mirror*, 'I don't know how he can possibly know so much about my sex life.' A year or two later, Lynne Franks, a mutual friend, dragged George over to talk to me at some Buddhist event I attended while working on a story for *The Face*. 'I only hated the book', he said, 'because it was all true.' In 1992, while recording the Pet Shop Boys-produced 'The Crying Game', he sent a message via Neil, saying that he'd never read the book before (which seemed highly unlikely) but now he had and really liked it. Still, when his own book, the excellent *Take It Like a Man*, came out in 1995, he couldn't resist a few digs. In one of these, he describes me in Japan as 'snooping', which made me laugh. What's a journalist supposed to do when invited to tour with a band? Hole up in his hotel room and ignore everything that's going on around him?

I spent the summer of 1985 working on a huge Duran Duran piece for *The Face*. I knew the band well through *Smash Hits*, and their press officer, the late Nick Underwood, was one of my closest friends. All the pieces were in place to do a piece of music writing properly for once, in true 'New Journalism' style – hang around with a band whenever they were doing something interesting, wait for the moments that were really revealing, observe and report. When it was published, of course, it was the same story as *Like Punk* . . . Everyone around Duran Duran loved the piece ('At last someone has written about it what it's really like,' said Michael Berrow, one of their managers) but the band themselves were cross. Nick Rhodes berated me for mentioning how much he'd spent on books one evening in New York, and an account of a dinner we had with Andy Warhol. 'It's just like tabloid journalism,' he complained. But how could I resist including dinner with Andy Warhol? And while he was talking, I was thinking, 'If only you knew the things that I knew about and didn't include in the piece . . .' By the end of that summer

I swear I could have told you Duran Duran's penis sizes in ascending order.

I came to the conclusion that pop stars felt, if they let you close to them, you would end up seeing them as they saw themselves. But of course, you don't. You end up seeing them the same way as all the other people who work with and around them. Having moved beyond the essentially benign *Smash Hits* context – I had stopped contributing to the magazine by autumn 1985 – in the end I felt I had to give up this kind of journalism altogether. It had become too emotionally difficult, embarking on a story knowing that at first it would be great and we'd all become friends, but that as soon as I wrote something that got close to the reality of a situation, they'd all hate me and never speak to me again.

The next phase of my life was a kind of detox from celebrity in Eastern Europe – I moved to Berlin in spring 1988. Sometime later that year, Bros were playing and a friend in the crew got me a pass. Incredibly, I walked in the backstage entrance to see the band splitting up right before my eyes – Craig Logan was whisked past me in a wheelchair after the final dressing-room row. I briefly considered filing a story somewhere, but decided to forget about it. My days as a pop journalist were over.

DAVE RIMMER

LIKE PUNK
NEVER
HAPPENED

INTRODUCTION

Imagine, for a moment, that you are a punk, hanging around the Roxy club in Covent Garden, sometime in early 1977. There you are in your ripped-up T-shirt, drainpipe jeans, brothel creepers and one of your dad's old suit jackets with the words 'No Future' daubed on the back. You've spiked up your newly-shorn hair with Vaseline and wrapped a studded dog collar, purchased that afternoon from Sam's Pet Supplies on the Essex Road and still with its lead attached, around your neck. It pinches a little but you can take it. Before coming out you have carefully festooned yourself with safety pins and in your hand – the final, essential touch – you clutch a can of lager.

It's only the second time you've been down the Roxy, and although it's still a bit scary you think it's great. The support band, Headbanger and the Nosebleeds, have just finished. They weren't very good but it didn't matter. You pogoed for a while and then chucked a few cans at them, which was much more fun than applauding would have been. Now, as you pose furiously near the fanzine sellers at the top of the stairs, you're satisfied that nothing will ever be the same again. The rock establishment is quaking in its boots, mate. Dinosaur acts like Queen, Pink Floyd, Genesis, Rod Stewart and Elton John won't be around for much longer, that's for certain. You'll see to that. New groups like Clash and Siouxsie and the Banshees will never sell out. The kids are in complete control now.

Suddenly, a strange figure pushes her way through the ragged, saucer-eyed, lager-clutching, bin-liner-bedecked throng. It looks like a sodding gypsy, you mutter to yourself, then realize with horror that she's heading for you.

' "No Future", dearie?' she cackles, producing a crystal ball from beneath her shawl. 'That's just where you're wrong. Cross my palm with silver and I'll *show* you the future.'

Overcome with curiosity, you slip her a ten pence piece and gaze, hypnotized, into the proffered globe.

It's horrible.

The stark, monochrome surrounds of the Roxy fade away into a distant hum as you are suddenly drawn into a procession of nightmarish scenes: pop stars dripping with pearls and swilling champagne, pop stars counting their money in long black limousines, pop stars bowing humbly to Prince Charles and chatting amiably to Terry Wogan on prime time television, pop stars – many of them familiar faces from the very club in which you are standing, transfixed – flying on Concorde and buying mansions around the world, *just like Elton John or Rod Stewart*!

With a hideous shriek, the gypsy snatches back the ball. ' "No Future", dearie? Just you wait and see,' she taunts and disappears into the crowd.

'It can't be true,' you keep telling yourself as you stumble past the cloakroom and out into the night to vomit violently in the gutter. 'It can't be true. It *can't* be. If that's the future then ... then ...

'It would be like punk never happened!'

This is the story of Culture Club, but it's also the story of pop music since punk. It's the story of how a generation of New Pop stars, a generation that had come of age during punk, absorbed its methods, learnt its lessons, but ditched its ideals – setting charts ablaze and fans screaming all over the world. It's the story of a whole new star system, of Adam Ant, Spandau Ballet, Duran Duran, Wham! and many others as well as Culture Club. It's also the story of a magazine called *Smash Hits*.

I've chosen to base this story round Culture Club because in many ways they were the perfect New Pop group. Only Michael Jackson was more famous than Boy George. *Colour By Numbers* was the nearest thing to a perfect pop album the decade has produced. 'Karma Chameleon' was the nearest thing to a perfect pop single: pretty and sickly, complex and singalong, meaningless and meaningful all at the same time, rising to number one in Britain, the USA and just about everywhere else where pop records are bought.

The only other group I could have written this story around would have been Duran Duran. Then there would maybe have been more about video, less about the press and dressing-up, but the essential details would have remained the same. In 1983, at the height of the New Pop period, Duran Duran and Culture Club were deadly rivals, but only different sides of the same coin.

As a writer for *Smash Hits* over this period – one which saw its circulation soar with the rise of the New Pop to become the world's biggest-selling pop magazine – I was allowed unusually close access. Unlike Fleet Street or the old music weeklies, *Smash Hits* was generally trusted not to 'slag people off' without good reason. I talked to, interviewed, travelled with, got to know and usually liked most of the New Pop stars. In writing this book, I'm not attempting to pass judgement on them, just to make some sense out of it all. And, I hope, make some money too.

In that sense, I'm as much a part of the New Pop – which is really the Old Pop now – as any of them.

THE BIRTH OF THE NEW POP

Picture the scene. It's a grey afternoon in early 1980. Jon Moss is sipping tea with Adam Ant and Marco Pirroni in the living room of a small Harrow semi-detached – Marco's parents' place. None of them are very famous yet. Oh, Jon was once voted 'the prettiest punk' in a fanzine and Adam's name gets sprayed on the backs of a few black leather jackets but that's about it. 'Cult,' Adam has decided, 'is just another word for loser.' Even the indignity of paying Malcolm McLaren £1000 for an intensive four-week attitude overhaul and then watching the former Sex Pistols manager walk off with his band hasn't softened Adam's resolve. Fired with fresh ideas, he's already recruited Marco Pirroni as a new collaborator and the pair are now looking for other musicians.

Jon Moss is also fed up with being a loser. A drummer, he's done time with them all – Damned, Clash, London, Jona Lewie, The Edge, Jane Aire and the Belvederes – but never managed to settle down with any of them. After spending three months staring blankly at his bedroom wall, he's just forked out £250 for an attitude overhaul of his own: a weekend Exegesis course. Although he came out of it a bit mad – thinking he could 'zap' things and change the colour of traffic lights and all that – he's determined to hit the big time now. Adam has approached him through an old girlfriend and this is their first meeting.

Mrs Pirroni flutters around excitedly offering everyone more tea. Adam munches a cupcake. Jon's finding all this a bit weird. Adam's so quiet and intense it's eery. He's almost robotic. He leans over to Jon and explains, 'I've got this idea for two drummers.' Out comes a tape of some Burundi drumming, part of a whole batch of stuff McLaren recorded for him. Jon listens, shrugs his shoulders and says, 'Okay, er, great.'

Two weeks later, Jon gets a call from Adam, loads his drum kit into the back of his estate car and drives down to Rockfield studio in Wales. He double tracks his playing to achieve a fair copy of the Burundi sound for Adam's last independent single, 'Cartrouble', bungs his drums back in the car and drives home. Jon gets a session fee but doesn't much fancy a full-time job with Marco and the mechanical man and Adam soon finds his two drummers elsewhere.

That was it really.

Except that eight months later Adam was topping the charts. And a few months after that the group McLaren stole from Adam and turned into Bow Wow Wow gave one George O'Dowd his first turn in front of a mike. And that it wasn't long before George, Jon and Culture Club were topping the charts too, along with Spandau Ballet, Wham!, Duran Duran and all the rest of the New Pop stars of the 1980s.

B̲ut Adam, in his own sweet way, was the very first of them all. In his rapid rise to the status of first teen idol of the 1980s, he mapped out all the moves for those who came after. Though the Human League and the Thompson Twins would later pull it off too, he was the first to engineer a self-conscious move from margins to mainstream, from cult to conqueror. He didn't seem to have even the tiniest prick of conscience about 'selling out' (an old hippy concept which the punks had adopted), he just made damn sure someone was buying. While the Clash were still making a self-righteous stand about never appearing on *Top Of The Pops* (not that by this time anyone wanted them to), Adam played the media for all he could get out of it. He ignored the traditional music press (*NME*, *Melody Maker*, etc.) which, in the late 1970s, had created both a vital lifeline and a deadly dull ghetto for the post-punk independent movement. They'd always slagged him off anyway. Instead he went straight to Fleet Street and the new glossies (*Smash Hits*, *The Face*). Taking a cue from Bowie and the Boomtown Rats (noted, at the time, for this sort of thing), he put a lot of effort, energy and imagination into his videos. Even if you didn't like the record, the latest clip was usually amusing. He gave up on the rock ideal and plunged himself into the idea of showbusiness, often verging on pantomime and at one point, around the time of 'Prince Charming', embracing it wholeheartedly. 'Such a new puritanism has grown up of late,' he told *The Face* in April 1981. 'I'd rather dress up like Liberace.' And then, of course, after the distinctly unsexy punk period, it was Adam who brought sex back into the equation. He talked about it almost as much as he talked about business (i.e. an awful lot), tattooed the words 'pure sex' on his arm and declared that he was making 'Ant Music for Sex People'.

With a single-mindedness bordering on obsession – in itself as characteristic of the New Pop as anything else Adam got up to – he became the first artist since the Sex Pistols successfully to sell, not just an unmistakeable 'look' (as he always put it) and an unmistakeable 'sound' (ditto), but also a half-baked set of theories and attitudes that pinned the two together. He'd dress up like Geronimo, play pop that leant heavily on African drumming and waffle on all the while about tribalism, the 'warrior ideal', noble savages and so forth. This was partly just a hangover from punk. 'Ideology had been important for so long,' noted writer Mary Harron, 'that it was hard to start a new fashion without one.' Spandau Ballet would have this same problem, and obviously a lot of what George did would beg some explanation, but groups like Duran Duran or Wham! never bothered to justify themselves at all – why should they? This was equally a measure of how much Adam had got from McLaren for his £1000, but most importantly it helped reinforce the idea of an Ant Clan as Adam gathered his fans around him and demanded not only their loyalty, but also a hefty slice of their pocket money.

Of course, much of what went into Adam's success had been done before and maybe better by other people. The Sex Pistols had the pop ideology to end them all (or so McLaren had hoped). T. Rex had made a similar move from margin to mainstream – in their case from dippy hippy fantasy folk duo to glam rock sensation – in the early 1970s. Scores of groups had worked hard on their videos. Adam never claimed to be original anyway. 'None of the ideas are mine,' he told *Smash Hits* in June 1981. 'It's just the way Marco and I have moulded them together.' He was talking about his music. The same, though, is true of his over all strategy. That he had a strategy at all is part of the point. That sort of thing had, in the past, usually been left up to managers and record companies.

'This is show business. That's two words. And if you don't take care of business, someone else is going to run your show.' The epigram isn't Adam's. It was coined by one David Grant, a British funk performer of fleeting renown. But really the words could have come from almost any British pop star of the last few years, Adam especially.

Adam was the punk who grew up wanting to own or control everything he did. He wrote, sang, recorded and performed all his own material. He designed his own sleeves and directed his own videos. When he revamped his look around 'Prince Charming' in the autumn of 1981, he patented the image through the Merchandizing Corporation of America and did his legal best to try and control every last sleeve, badge, T-shirt, poster or sticker bearing his face or his name. That he had to pay photographers to use their pictures of the image he'd created, he regarded as scandalous. He once remarked that he never touched alcohol because 'if you drink a lot of people take advantage of you'. During his heyday, Adam's publishers would demand of *Smash Hits* more than twice the going rate for the right to reproduce one of his lyrics. Adam's explanation: 'That's business.'

And so it was.

And so it would be for all the New Pop groups who followed. In the 1960s the Beatles lost millions through inept management and pirate merchandizing. Now groups started setting up merchandizing and publishing companies almost before they'd played a gig. A good business head was suddenly more important than the ability to play an instrument, though that helped too. People no longer mistrusted record companies because they might mess with their artistic integrity; they simply worried that they might not be able to sell enough of their records.

'Don't bother me with all your "arty" stuff,' grunted Adam. 'I live in the nitty-gritty world.'

Ironically, it may well have been Adam's habit of impressing his business acumen on all and sundry that led to, if not his downfall, then at least his departure from the dizzy heights he achieved in 1981 and 1982. After a while, behind the make-up and the costumes and the star-studded videos, even his fans began to perceive the same monomaniacal success robot that Jon Moss had shared a cupcake or two with back in early 1980.

Spin the wheel, watch it turn. Rock and roll in 1956, beat and the Beatles in 1963, hippies and psychedelia in 1967, Bowie and Roxy and glam rock in 1972, punk in 1976 . . . watch it turn. As an old wave degenerates and expires, so a new wave explodes and regenerates. Every five years or so the paradigms shift. So runs the cyclical theory of pop and so, after punk, we get the New Pop. Simple, isn't it?

Well, up to a point. This cyclical game is supposed to hinge on a delicate balance between art and business, between expression and exploitation. Very glibly: in a consumer society, you are what you buy. As you choose what you spend your money on – within the limits both of what's on offer and of what you can afford – you choose what you *are*. If you buy crushed velvet flares, a long string of beads, some marijuana and a pile of records that are all about going to San Francisco and wearing flowers in your hair, then you're a hippy, right? If you buy bondage strides, a packet of safety-pins, some Crazy Colour, a copy of 'Anarchy In The UK' and a large tube of modelling glue, then you're a punk. In a *perfect moment* everything clicks together. The records you buy are by people who dress the same way that you do and express themselves in a manner that sums up the way you feel about things, too. A whole generation, artists *and* audience, thinks that

11

going to San Francisco and festooning itself with daffodils to the tune of Jefferson Airplane's 'White Rabbit', or going to the Rainbow Theatre, and ripping up the seats to the tune of the Clash playing 'White Riot' is exactly the right thing to be doing. And if your parents don't like it, well, that's precisely the point. That's your perfect moment.

But of course it stops being perfect as soon as money starts being made. The artists get altogether too concerned with business and disappear off to distant mansions. The people who've been buying their records realize that they've ceased to express themselves and are simply being exploited. The artists all start writing concept albums and the public all throw their crushed velvet flares in the bin and go off to get proper jobs. The result is a bit of cultural vacuum and, since nature abhors this, sooner or later the Next Big Thing comes rushing along to fill it up. Raw, young, vital and local, it is immediately taken up by the younger brothers and sisters of the last lot.

And that's how the wheel spins.

Or so the theory goes.

In fact, outside the general notion that there's always both a younger crowd eager to consume something different from their forebears and a younger bunch of bands eager to cater for them, the only phenomenon it makes any sense of at all is punk. Sure, before punk there'd been shifts and changes aplenty – many of them dramatic enough – but the only other time the commercial rationale of it all had been even vaguely called into question was during the hippy era. We are now further from punk than punk was from Woodstock, and though in the intervening years there have been a myriad cults, fads and revivals, there still hasn't been an explosion as such. If those who insist that the importance of youth is dying with the decline of teenage spending power are right, there will be no new explosion ever again.

All of which begs the question of the New Pop. It didn't burst out, it just grew slowly: first a spark, then a smoulder and before you knew it the whole house was on fire. In the absence of an explosion, our theory would dismiss the whole phenomenon as unworthy of serious consideration. But in cold commercial terms, at the very least, as British pop groups began to conquer charts and minds all over the world and London once again came to be seen from afar as some kind of thriving capital of youth

12

culture, there had been nothing so spectacular since the Beatles. Many complain that the youth explosion of the 1960s was a damn sight more significant and 'authentic' than all this mass-marketed pop for the video age. Maybe they're right. But try telling that to a 15-year-old Culture Club fan whose life has never been the same since George replied to one of her letters.

The irony of the situation is this: to those who cling on to the spirit of punk, everything about the New Pop is utterly abhorrent and devoid of their precious 'credibility'. The New Pop isn't rebellious. It embraces the star system. It conflates art, business and entertainment. It cares more about sales and royalties and the strength of the dollar than anything else and to make matters worse, it isn't the least bit guilty about it.

It is, in short, like punk never happened. But if the spark that set the New Pop smouldering came from anywhere, it came from punk.

'We all trace our roots back to one of the early Sex Pistols gigs,' Gary Kemp told me in summer 1982, shortly before Spandau Ballet made the transition to a life of limousines, stadium concerts, *Sun* exclusives and antique collecting. He was talking about all the new British groups that were then in and around the charts: Human League, ABC, Duran Duran, Haircut One Hundred, Adam Ant. Doubtless most would have agreed with him. 'That's where it all really started. Our ideas were got together and formulated in 1979, but it was all based on things we'd picked up as we went along from those early punk days when I was only sixteen . . .'

In the beginning, the most obvious thing Spandau had picked up was a business lesson. Their manager Steve Dagger's skilful steering of the group from club set to charts owed more than a nod to the business strategy Malcom McLaren had gleefully set in motion with the Sex Pistols and later turned into the parable of 'The Ten Lessons' in the film *The Great Rock 'n' Roll Swindle*. No matter that McLaren was motivated as much by making trouble as by making money. Dagger had been paying attention, and it worked well either way.

If Adam was the first of the artists as businessmen then McLaren was the businessman as artist. He didn't play the guitar, but he did play the media. More interested in an adventure than a career, he was in some respects an awful manager. He just didn't care. No good going to him if you were looking for a future in the pop game. He'd drop you as soon as he got bored. 'It wouldn't have mattered if Annabella (of Bow Wow Wow) had gone under a bus,' he remarked in 1984, playing the rogue bit up to the hilt. 'We could have replaced her.' His troublemaking was effective, though, and it's remarkable how long and large his influence has loomed. Leaving aside Dagger and all the others who learnt by his example, McLaren's own c.v. is impressive enough.

He reinvented Adam so successfully that he topped the pop heap for two years. He invented Bow Wow Wow who, although they don't look such hot property in the cold light of hindsight, seemed in 1981 (along with Adam and Spandau) to embody much of the spirit of the times: a splash of colour and bravado amid the gathering gloom of the British depression. He was the first to spot the star potential of George O'Dowd and gave him a crucial leg up into the limelight. For better or worse he pioneered the idea of cultural plunder and helped bring the hip-hop/break dance culture to Britain with his 1983 hit 'Buffalo Gals'. And in making his *Duck Rock* solo LP with Trevor Horn, he inspired the star producer to unearth a lot of the ideas, influences and noises that would later go into making Frankie Goes To Hollywood the pop sensation that would really turn the whole thing full circle.

But punk was McLaren's finest hour. As co-owner (with Vivienne Westwood) of the King's Road clothes shop Sex (later Seditionaries, later still all sorts of things) and as manager of the Sex Pistols, he spearheaded a movement that aimed, not to spin the wheel, but to shove a bloody great spanner in the spokes. With the maximum of ceremony, punk dealt the remnants of the 1960s rock establishment a good ideological kicking which, if it didn't make them go away, at least left them smarting. Record companies, radio stations and the music press were all caught high and dry. Old hippies everywhere suddenly found themselves not only out of date, but openly despised.

McLaren was of course neither the first nor the last imaginative entrepreneur to make the most out of an easily manipulable music industry, but he was probably the first to make a show out of doing it. In the death, which came quickly, the Pistols were always more of a media event than, in the classic sense, a rock group and their business dealings were as much a part of the act as Rotten's sneer or Sid stubbing a fag out on his arm. It might have been nothing more than a few swear words on the telly that got the Pistols sacked from two major record labels but, as they waltzed off, giggling, with a couple of fat cheques, they used the glare of scandal to illuminate the workings of a by now extremely jittery music industry for all to see.

Having lit the blue touchpaper, the Pistols retired with a court case (Rotten *v.* McLaren) and a martyr (Sid Vicious) and left what remained of the great rock 'n' roll myth for the Clash to go chasing after. While Sid was mourned by those poor souls who refused to believe that punk had died, Rotten changed his name back to Lydon and gave us a taste of things to come. He named his new group, Public Image Limited, as though it was a business.

Punk left behind it a few star groups (Clash, Jam, Police), a few new music businessmen (Miles Copeland, Bernard Rhodes) and a whole generation of teenagers who'd been inspired to believe that they too could start their own band, work the business and find fame and fortune. Gary Kemp again: 'I was sixteen at the time and believed that to be in a band you had to live in Hollywood, have incredible amounts of money and be an unbelievably brilliant musician. But punk had said all that was rubbish.' This wasn't just pie in the sky. Conditions had changed. Having failed to make much money out of punk and determined not to be caught out again, the music industry began looking in earnest for marketable young talent. On the other hand, the young talent had learnt a deep distrust of the music business and approached it warily. They were no longer so naïve. They were no longer about to let themselves be exploited.

Also determined never to be caught out again was the British music press. More widely read and more influential in Britain than anywhere else in the world, the music press – consisting, in the late 1970s, of the four weeklies *Melody Maker*, *Sounds*, *Record Mirror* and the *NME* – had been 'favourite colour' fan magazines in the 1950s and 1960s, found a more adult footing in the hippy days and were beginning to flounder a bit by the mid-1970s. Once they'd caught on to punk, which took them a while, it turned out to be a godsend. Here was something that *needed* them, needed explaining and interpreting, something that actually looked good in gritty black-and-white on smudgy newsprint. How nice it was to be important again. Once punk went the way of all flesh, they too began casting around for the Next Big Thing. If it happened, they were going to be the ones to let you know about it. In fact, they'd let you know about anything, just in case.

There were plenty of candidates, though no one was sure how seriously to take them. Stylistically, punk had thrown bits of every post-war subculture up in the air. In the uncertain climate that followed, it all began to fall back to earth as marketable 'revivals'. Over the next few years there were to appear revamped versions of ted, rockabilly, skinhead, hippy, beatnik, mod and even, after a scarcely decent interval, punk. All came with their own groups and most, of course, involved attempted hypes by lesser McLarens with some kind of vested interest.

First off the block was the mod revival. A joke for the most part, consisting as it did at first of unimaginative Jam imitators in parkas, it did manage to spawn 2-Tone. This was a Coventry independent label, rooted in a punky version of ska and centred round Jerry Dammers' group, the Specials. After scoring one independent hit, they came to a model arrangement with Chrysalis records. Instead of just signing the band, Chrysalis signed the label too. 2-Tone signed the bands, decided on the releases, provided the distinctive black-and-white artwork; Chrysalis provided the bankroll, and got the records into the shops. Not only did this result in a whole crop of new groups (Madness and The Beat among them) and some fine singles, but everyone concerned also made a lot of money. At a time when record sales in Britain were dropping by 20 per cent and when EMI and Decca – for thirty years the two dominant British companies – did so badly they were both taken over, that wasn't bad going. It was beginning to seem as though the artists knew better than the companies.

Though certainly the most successful, 2-Tone wasn't the only high profile independent label. Hundreds sprang up between 1977 and 1980. Some, like Stiff, were smaller, more imaginative versions of the major companies. Some, like Zoo in Liverpool or Factory in Manchester, were formed to reflect a local musical identity – after London-based punk it was a time when Britain's other major cities began to assert themselves. Most were tiny concerns formed by individual groups to release their own records. 'Do-it-yourself' was the dictum and if punk had said you didn't have to be a brilliant musician or live in Hollywood to be in a band, it also implied that you didn't need to spend a small fortune on recording costs, packaging or marketing to release a record. Or

16

at least, not if you were happy with sales of up to 20,000. For more than that you really did have to start spending money again.

For a time, though, most independent groups were happy with small sales. A spirit of experimentation reigned. The movement – it soon became one with its own 'alternative' shops, clubs, charts and distribution network – was idealistic, committed, questioning and, of course, the music press loved it. Here was something that needed them, not just to be explained, but simply to survive. Without exposure in the *NME* and on John Peel's national Radio 1 show, the independent labels would have died very quickly. Most of them did anyway. In this sense, with the volume of press coverage far outstripping hard record sales (a group could find themselves on the cover of the *NME* after releasing, say, one 5000-seller single – often a problem for groups on the dole) the independent movement was even more of a media event than punk.

Money was the death of it, of course. While the major companies operate by handing a group a large advance against future sales, the independents would split costs and profits 50/50 with the groups. That meant that if you didn't spend much and sold moderately, you could make a living. If you sold well, you could make a killing, which is precisely what UB40 and Depeche Mode did. They were lucky. The trouble was, to sell well you needed to spend a lot on advertising and promotion. If that didn't work, a group could wind up with 50 per cent of a massive debt to pay and no money to make the next record. This became an incentive to mediocrity. Wary of trying to make a big splash, groups just concentrated on keeping their heads above water.

Coupled with the punk amateur ethic, this quickly led the independents into a stylistic ghetto. While able to be as esoteric as they wanted without having to worry about paying back an advance, groups were limited by small budgets and lack of technical skill. The dour, gloomy style of Joy Division and Echo and the Bunnymen, who were actually very good at it, soon became the norm, while others found self-conscious experimentation to be a bit of a dead end.

'In retrospect it is hard to take stock of it,' Green of Scritti Politti – a group once so fiercely committed to the independent ethic that they used to print a breakdown of production costs on all their sleeves – told me in 1982. 'I mean, going down to the Electric Ballroom and hitting empty film cans and scratching a guitar about, playing this jittering, apologetic half-reggae and singing about hegemony while putting in as many discords as you could was probably doomed to failure, I suppose.'

Indeed.

The charts were full of glossy disco and polished soul and the lure of the lavish high-tech production was hard to resist after the penny-pinching practice of the independents. Who'd want to suffer the unglamorous task of packing thousands of copies of their new single by hand when everything that pop had ever promised lurked tantalizingly just around the corner. After a single or two, the more ambitious and commercial groups, usually now armed with a following of sorts and a crucial understanding of the mechanics of the business, began fleeing to the major labels. The Human League, for example, signed to Virgin, announced that they wanted to be like Abba, and clung on to their 'synthesizers only' policy because, singer Philip Oakey explained, 'we don't want musicians coming in and doing things we're not directly controlling every bit of'. Scritti Politti took a year off, polished up their act and returned with a new member who, although he appeared in photographs, didn't sing, play an instrument or do anything at all on stage. He simply organized their business affairs.

The independents soon began to flounder. Many died. Others brought their practices more into line with the major labels. Rough Trade, one of the biggest and most important, was forced to lay off a number of its staff in 1983 and now signs groups – like The Smiths, with whom they've had considerable success – on an advance/royalty basis. The independents survived as long as they did in a time of recession by catering for what Factory boss Tony Wilson called 'the kids for whom music means more than money'. But times were changing.

In May 1979, a young man called Gary Numan armed with a battery of synthesizers, a batch of Bowie's old movies and an armful of adolescent angst-ridden songs scored a number one hit with his single, 'Are "Friends" Electric'. Before long he'd been successful enough to form his own company, employ most of his family and invest the profits of his art in all manner of business. He numbered a fleet of aeroplanes, a mansion in Virginia Water, a hovercraft, a helicopter, a racing car and a restaurant franchise among his rapidly accumulated assets. 'Originally I wanted to be

18

famous like I wanted to breathe,' he sighed after becoming the
first rock star ever to fly around the world. 'Now I just want to
be rich.'

It wasn't just Numan's balding business head that fore-
shadowed things to come. While the independents had been sol-
diering worthily along, a new, younger teenage market was beginning to emerge. The younger brothers and sisters of the punks,
they preferred Blondie or the Police to the Clash or the Stranglers
and never took punk very seriously. Numan suited them perfectly.
He looked good, his make-up and black clothes were easy to copy,
you could dance to the music and wring some slight significance
out of the words. While the older fans were finding jobs hard to
come by, the younger ones had pocket money to spend. They
spent a lot of it on Numan.

The music press absolutely hated him, spat every drop of
venom they could in his direction. He was shallow, second-hand
and committed to nothing other than his own success. It didn't
hurt him a bit. His fans didn't read the music press with its ever-
lengthening, academic editorial and arty photos. In autumn 1978
Smash Hits, a new fortnightly magazine, was launched. It was
full of glossy colour pictures, song lyrics and covered both punk
and disco brightly and informatively. Its sales immediately began
to outstrip the competition. The staples of *Smash Hits* weren't
the doomy northern independent bands, but people who looked
good in colour: Numan, Blondie, Police, Toyah. It cared nothing
for political commitment or artistic integrity. It cared about the
charts.

The wheel was turning again. The 1970s were preparing their
last gasp.

Picture another scene. It's a rainy
Tuesday night in early 1980. At the Blitz wine bar in Covent
Garden, one of Steve Strange and Rusty Egan's weekly 'Heroes'
Nights' is in full swing. They moved here a while ago from Billy's
in Soho and business is beginning to thrive. Looking around you
can see punks and art students and soul boys and transvestites

and freelance oddballs all dressed, not necessarily to kill, but definitely to be noticed. Around the edges of the throng shuffles the odd nervous freelance photographer, snapping randomly in the hope that this will turn out to be the Next Big Thing. On the door, former shop assistant turned professional socialite Steve Strange hopes so, too, which is why he's let them in. The media are just beginning to hear about this place and all *paparazzi* are welcomed, but most sightseers, except maybe the odd film director Strange wants to suck up to, get short shrift.

The scene is bewildering at first. Such a cacophony of styles, as many different 'looks' as there are layers of make-up. But as you get used to the place, it's possible to discern various distinct factions. There, by the front end of the bar, so positioned because they're among the few who can afford to buy drinks, are a clique of what Peter York christened Thems: artists Andrew Logan and Duggie Fields and a couple of passing models. Film director Derek Jarman and fashion designer Jasper Conran are upstairs in the restaurant. Further down the bar are some characters from the artier end of punk. Billy Idol, maybe, and Siouxsie Sioux; sometimes even Chrissie Hynde of the Pretenders. This is just another club as far as they're concerned. Somewhere to hang out now the Vortex has closed down. Midge Ure and Rusty Egan will soon wander over to join them for a drink.

Strategically positioned at the top of the toilet stairs, midway between the bar and the dance floor, is the North London 'soul boy' crowd. Steve Dagger and Gary Kemp and most of Spandau Ballet are here, although few beyond the Blitz regulars have heard of them yet. In fact, the room is packed with people who are about to become famous – as designers or writers or musicans or hat-makers or whatever. For the time being they are content with just dressing up and pretending to be famous.

Over there, for example, in the back of this dingy little club, by the cloakroom. This is where the crowd from the Warren Street squat hang out: Marilyn and Andy Polaris and Jeremy Healey. In a year or two they'll all have their own recording contracts, but these days they're still passing the job of cloakroom attendant between them, depending on who most needs the money that week. Tonight it's the turn of George O'Dowd. George isn't that much more flamboyant than the rest of the crowd but he's certainly a lot louder and his sharp tongue has earned him enemies

as well as friends. He and the North London crowd, for example, haven't been on speaking terms for years. There are those who say he nicks money from the coat pockets. Indeed, there are those who say he nicks the coats. Jasper Conran is still looking for one he left there the other week.

Though not uniformly liked, George is certainly well known. He's a fixture. This crowd's main aim in life is dressing up and getting their pictures in the papers as often as possible and George is very good at it. So good, in fact, that he'll still be doing it years after most of this bunch have packed away their pan-stick and velvet knickerbockers for good.

'In the future,' once quipped that great-grandaddy of all pop businessmen, Andy Warhol, 'everyone will be famous for fifteen minutes.' This epigram was quoted to clichédom years ago, but the new romantics took it to heart. Punk had applied the anyone-can-do-it idea to the process of forming a band and becoming famous; the new romantics ditched the trappings and applied it to fame, pure and simple. Forming a band came later. Spandau Ballet were the first to do it, dragging the whole scene into the limelight with them. For a while new romanticism – there were lots of labels but that one came the closest to sticking – was held up to be the genuine article: the authentic Next Big Thing. Since the early 1970s, the soul clubs had fostered a whole series of 'looks' – the Bowie/Ferry wedge look, the Badlands 1950s look, the billowing bags and braces old man's look, the Glen Miller look – but it wasn't until punk alerted the media to the possibility of a resurgent underground that anyone began paying attention. With new romantic they began making up for lost airtime and showered the Blitz crowd in a storm of picture features and pop sociology overviews.

But it never really took off. The new romantic notion was too confused to sweep the nation. Punk style might have dismembered bits of every post-war fashion, but it put them all back together in a kind of collage that became a definite, marketable 'look'. The new romantics took the mix 'n' match approach further back in history, further afield in the globe. But as they spent their entire time trying to outdo each other – 'Oh *dear!*' George would be heard putting someone down, '*Nobody* ever wears the same thing two weeks running!' – a distinct look never really emerged. In early 1981, as the movement went fully public, there was a brief trade in frilly shirts but that was about as far as it went.

It wasn't the only reason the fad never caught on. The fact that everyone spent their entire time angrily disavowing whatever label anyone tried to thrust upon them – 'Blitz Kids', 'Futurists', 'The New Dandies' and even 'The Cult With No Name' – didn't help. It was hard enough trying to be a new romantic in, say, Grantham, without the person whose clothes you were trying to copy saying that they certainly were *not* a new romantic, thank you very much. The only group who ever embraced the term, and then only briefly, were Duran Duran who came from Birmingham, and therefore, as far as the London lot were concerned, didn't know any better.

The lack of great pop singles didn't help either. Spandau's 'To Cut A Long Story Short' or Duran's 'Planet Earth' were OK debut singles, but they were hardly the stuff to fire the imagination of a generation of young musicians and, sure enough, didn't. Even in the early 1981 heyday of it all, there were never more than a handful of bands that could be identified as new romantic and most of them had died before the year was out. The great pop singles were to come later.

But for all that new romantic was important. By defining itself in opposition to everything 'grey and boring', it effectively killed off all but the best of the Northern doomy bands. Through its relentless eclecticism, it opened a way for all manner of music that had previously been kept at arm's length from the by now ailing rock tradition: Latin, African, even jazz and disco. In the short term it breathed new life into the idea of the club: the 12-inch single instead of the live group, with the audience as the stars. Soon London would have the massive Camden Palace and every other major British city would have something smaller but similar. It let loose a whole flood of young designers, photographers, writers and would-be musicians.

But most importantly, it bridged the gap between what had hitherto been two opposing traditions – punk and disco – and in so doing created the conditions for a whole new mainstream. Club culture didn't just sow the seeds for Culture Club, it paved the way for the biggest pop explosion since the 1960s.

Business was about to boom.

FOUR BOYS

GEORGE

New Year's Eve, 1984, and at the door of the White Trash club in London's Piccadilly, the final few minutes of the year are ticking away into a near riot. Doorperson Fat Tony has decided not to let anyone else in. A forest of invitations is being waved in his face, but he doesn't care: they shall not pass. In the long, narrow corridor that leads up to the entrance, an increasingly turbulent crowd of London's brighter young things are pushing and shoving and shouting and trying their damnedest not to take no for an answer. Some of them actually seem to be enjoying the situation. Things are getting ugly.

Weary of the crush, I've left my companions to it and am now standing out on the pavement, watching the crowds flow towards Trafalgar Square and wishing I was anywhere but

25

London. Then, round the corner, clad in some long black garment with his newly-shorn hair dyed bright yellow and purple, comes Boy George.

'Hello,' I smile, surprised and pleased to see him. 'Happy new year!'

George just glares at me. A scowl, blacker than the night, spreads across his face. 'Hello-how-are-you,' he grunts in a tone that invites no reply, then turns sharply away.

The clock strikes twelve, Fat Tony comes out and opens a side door especially for George and about thirty people promptly try to follow him through it. My friends give up the queue and we hop in a cab to another party. The encounter has left me perplexed. Everything I've ever written about Culture Club has annoyed George one way or another but – apart from the occasional bitchy note or semi-serious ticking off – he's never been anything less than friendly when we've met. Now it seems that, having heard I'm working on this book, George has decided to get annoyed with me in advance, just in case.

War might, as the song says, be stupid, but having wars with people seems to be one of George's ways of tackling situations he's not sure of. He had a war, for example, with his old friend Jeremy Healey in 1982. Culture Club and Jeremy's group Haysi Fantayzee had set out simultaneously, both with a dreadlocked look that caused the media to bracket them together. This annoyed George, but he soon established a distance. He had a war with another old friend, Marilyn, when, after the pair returned from their much-publicized Egyptian holiday together, Marilyn launched his solo career with a barrage of publicity based on his association with George. Having a war allows George to keep something problematic at arm's length until the situation naturally sorts itself out or he's decided how to deal with it. Which is what he seems to be doing with me and this book.

Wars are also just an extension of George's naturally extremely argumentative temperament. He often talks in interviews about

26

his need for arguments, his hot temper and his dislike of other people who show no strong emotion. In those same interviews he nearly always appears to be a bright, funny, friendly, down-to-earth and extremely likeable sort of a bloke. Which is precisely what he is – about half of the time. When he's in a bad mood he's rude, ratty, intolerant, perfectly vile to everyone around him and so sharp-tongued that he can reduce people to tears. This side of him only comes out occasionally in public, with the odd punch-up with a Fleet Street photographer or the occasional slanging match with another celebrity. 'George always gets pissed off when he meets someone more famous than he is,' Jon told me once.

It was a pertinent observation, because George enjoys his rows almost as much as he enjoys being world famous. That is to say, rather a lot. His relationships, even – maybe especially – with those to whom he is closest, are characterized by often quite violent rows. He and Jon Moss, for example, seem to fight all the time. When Jon broke his finger and most of Culture Club's autumn 1983 British tour had to be postponed, the official story from the group was that Jon had fallen over on the tour bus. The rumour, which seemed more likely, was that he'd injured it in a fight with George.

Above all, George is quick-tempered. He can swing from one extreme to the other at the drop of his Hasidic hat. So difficult is a bad-tempered George to work with, that reports on his moods circulate furtively around his entourage. 'It's all right,' I remember everyone saying to each other one potentially awkward morning on tour, 'George was singing as he got up today.' The relief was palpable.

George seems always to have needed rows to relate to people. He was born George Alan O'Dowd on 14 June 1961, the third son in an Irish Catholic South London family that would in time be further expanded with two more sons and one daughter. In the O'Dowd household, rows were a way of life. Conditions, with six children, two adults and two large dogs in one small three-bedroomed house, were cramped. George's father, Jeremiah, was a builder with a struggling business and, George remembers, he 'used to come back and take his aggression out on us because he'd had a hard day at work'. The eldest son, Richard, was a tearaway who frequently got into trouble with the police. With pressures like that on the family, coupled with having to fight for attention as the middle child in such a large brood, it's not surprising that George became a very difficult and argumentative youngster. His tales of childhood revolve around extreme rows and violent emotions: George throwing his dinner on the floor, his mother throwing the toaster at him, George screaming, 'I hate you, I hate you', his father chasing him up the stairs and kicking down the bathroom door. That last fight, George told me, began because he'd brought home a nude picture he'd found in a skip. As his father smashed in the door, George tripped and cut himself. As his father calmed down and wondered, 'God, what have I done?', George ran out of the house and went to stay at a friend's for two weeks. When he came back, his father had changed and the pair of them never rowed in quite the same way again.

The desire for fame seems to go back as far as the need for war. I once asked George what his earliest memory was. 'My *very* earliest memories have been conveniently erased,' he replied. 'You know, sandcastles and falling off your bike and stuff. The only thing I can remember distinctly are the train journeys I used to take from suburbia into the West End. I would always look out over the buildings and say to myself that it was very sad that I'd never know all the people who lived in them. Or more to the point, that they'd never know me.'

His need to be noticed began to manifest itself early. When he was eleven, his aunt Josie brought round a bag of clothes for Mrs O'Dowd to go through. 'There was this big flared lurex catsuit,' George remembers. 'Really hideous. And I sneaked it out of the front room and took it in at the waist so it would fit me. I never wore it out. Maybe to the front garden but that was about as daring as I could be.'

In his early teens, fired by an obsession with Marc Bolan, George began wearing embroidered jackets and turning his trousers into flares with huge velvet inserts. On one well-documented occasion, he went to Sunday school in massive flares, platform shoes, a cravat, a camel-hair coat and a huge floppy hat. By the age of fourteen he'd fallen in with a girl called Tracy Burch. The pair of them scoured Oxfam shops, stole from more expensive boutiques and employed gallons of dye, their mothers' sewing machines and a lot of imagination to put together their own unique outfits.

George was now turning up at school with a 'trowel' haircut, coloured whatever gaudy hue had taken his fancy that week, drainpipe trousers, white plastic sandals, collarless shirts and a school tie cut in half and sewn smaller by his obliging mother. Naturally, it didn't go down too well. Under the regime of headmaster Peter Dawson, Eltham Green was a tough school. George's uncompromising sartorial stance coupled with his utter lack of respect for teachers and his 'perpetual truancy' soon found him doodling away his days in the remedial class, supervised by a psychologist. After bunking off once too often, he refused the cane and found himself expelled at the age of fifteen. As the *Sunday Times* would later note rather snootily, his school career ended with an academic record 'unblemished by achievement'.

The year was 1976 and 'unblemished by achievement' could equally have described the music of the day. Glam rock had sparked up the early 1970s for those too young to have been hippies or, like George's elder brother, skinheads. For a while, Marc Bolan, Gary Glitter, Sweet and a host of other glam trash acts – including Alice Cooper and Lou Reed from across the Atlantic – had flourished in a cloud of glitter. By now they had withered and died and left only two figures for anyone to identify with: Bryan Ferry and David Bowie. It's hard for anyone not in Britain and involved at the time to understand how important those two were. It was partly musical. Bowie and Roxy Music were the only wedge between British pomp rock on the one side and bland Americana on the other. They could be danced to in the ballroom and then concentrated upon in the thoughtful adolescent's bedroom. It was partly sartorial. They introduced a generation to a world of clothes and a way of dressing up in them that went beyond the simple duplication of a specified 'look'. It was partly a matter of boundaries. They were a point where the rock crowd and the disco set intersected. All these things were influential enough still to be reverberating as the next decade came along. At the time they also, Bowie in particular, provoked a questioning of sex roles, and gave a lot of those who came up with difficult answers the courage to say them out loud.

George was a classic Bowie kid. He went to see him at Earl's Court in 1973. He and all his friends were among the crowd that greeted Bowie at Victoria station in May 1976 on his arrival back in Britain after a two-year absence. 'You didn't realize how many weird people there were till you went,' George remembers. Like

29

many Bowie kids, George hadn't just dyed his hair, he'd also decided he was gay. He talked about it to his father who was unruffled. He talked to his friends about it, incessantly. Now he says: 'I don't believe people should live their sexuality.' Then, he was just beginning to find out about it.

With a group of friends who, for some reason, called themselves Arnolds, he began to venture further afield than the local discos and up to gay clubs in the West End. Bangs, Louise's, Chaguarama's and the Global Village were places they'd trek to. George began sleeping around a bit. Among the other suburban gangs hitting the same spots in town was the Bromley contingent, led by Siouxsie and Billy Idol.

Punk was just beginning to bite. Through a friend, George landed a £6-a-day job at a King's Road clothes shop named Shades. He and owner Troy, it is said, invented the tartan bondage trouser. The King's Road soon became a battle ground between punks and teds. George pitched his personal style somewhere between the two – often appearing with a huge quiff and a painted-on moustache – which seemed to bring him trouble from both camps.

He was beginning to make firm friends. On the bus to work he met Jeremy Healey. At a club called Bangs he spotted this bloke wearing a skirt, a black paper collar, horns, leather gloves, black lipstick and pit boots. Then he saw him again in Louise's, this time clad in a top hat, suspenders, shorts and a jacket with Malteser wrappers all over it. This was Philip Sallon, the inveterate poseur-about-town. He quickly became both a firm friend and a big influence on George. Another new extravagantly-dressed crony was Martin Degville, later to make his name as one of the early designers parading under the banner of the new romantics.

But George wasn't too happy in London. After work at Shades dried up, he tried Tesco, only to be sacked after a week for the way he dressed. He also fell out with Philip. So George moved up to Birmingham for a while, sharing a flat with Martin Degville and others and having a whale of a time on the then quite lively Birmingham circuit. He and Martin would gad about clubs like Barbarella's and the Holy City Zoo, getting ever more outrageous as they vied to outdo each other. 'We were like the ugly sisters,' says George, who had begun going out with a red neck, blue face and mauve hair.

George found Birmingham relaxing, but after a year moved back down to London, bolder and brasher than ever. His crowd had now expanded to include Andy Polaris – later to be singer with Animal Nightlife – and one Peter Robinson, a 'right little wally' of a soul boy who suddenly, with the aid of a dress, a padded bra, crimped hair and false eyelashes, transformed himself into Marilyn. They'd all begun hanging round in a Soho dive called Billy's every Friday night, and George spread the word about this new haunt far and wide. People remember him raving about it at Bowie's Earl's Court concert in 1978.

One of the other Bowie kids who began spending his Friday nights at Billy's was Rusty Egan, erstwhile drummer with the Rich Kids, a post-punk group that included Midge Ure and former Sex Pistol Glen Matlock but got absolutely nowhere. Egan and one David Claridge – these days the man behind TV-AM's Roland Rat – had the bright idea of taking over the club on Tuesdays for the now legendary 'Bowie Nights'. The pair would play some electronic and some funky dance music, but mostly just Bowie. It proved a popular idea. So popular that one night, in an attempt to control the numbers flooding in, Egan asked his shop assistant flatmate, Steve Strange, to mind the door. Which is how their partnership began. And, of course, among the early overdressed crowd at Billy's, mingling with a host of future designers, writers and pop musicians, were Jeremy, Philip Sallon, Marilyn, Andy Polaris and George. After five months, Billy's was so crowded that Strange and Egan began looking around for another venue. They found Blitz.

By this time George had moved out of his parents' place in Shooters Hill and into a squat near Kentish Town tube station. Marilyn, Andy Polaris and a girl called Mad Myra moved in too. Despite troubles with the local skinheads and problems with the electricity supply, they stuck it out until finding another squat in Great Titchfield Street in the West End. This place had no kitchen but was otherwise ideal: it was only a short walk from all the clubs.

Blitz was booming and the media were beginning to take notice. Life for George and his crew was damn near perfect. Now they not only dressed up and went out all the time, they also began getting their pictures in the papers. Some of those people in the houses George had once looked out at wonderingly from the train, were now picking up their Sunday papers and looking wonderingly at a bejewelled and greasepaint-covered George. Fame was beginning to beckon.

The squat in Great Titchfield Street was abandoned and a large Victorian house in nearby Carburton Street was taken over instead. The occupants now also included a rockabilly photographer called Paranoid Pete and Miss Binnie, a woman who performed in a nude, body-painting cabaret troupe called the Neo-Naturists and was fond of organizing assorted bizarre parties and events. Another squat round the corner in Warren Street housed an assortment of nightclubbing art and fashion students including Stephen Linard, John Maybury, Melissa Caplan and George's old friend Jeremy Healey.

George worked for a while in a hat shop before being sacked for turning up in a kilt. He earned some cash through the Peter Benison modelling agency, an organization that provides 'youth types' for adverts and the like. A representative of their 'new weirdo side', George featured in ads for British Airways and the Trustee Savings Bank. He was also picking up a few bob doing the cloakroom at Blitz. His dress was getting ever more outrageous – he'd be Carmen Miranda one night, Boadicea the next and Mary Magdalen the night after that – and his picture was appearing in the papers with increasing regularity.

One night at a club called Planets, where Philip Sallon was running Thursday nights, George brought himself to the attention of Malcolm McLaren. He'd heard that McLaren was trying out different singers for a Bow Wow Wow event at the Rainbow theatre, and flounced up to the manager wearing stilettoes and a large straw hat with birds on it. 'I want to sing with Bow Wow Wow,' he announced drunkenly. McLaren couldn't see why not.

George now reckons McLaren only used him to frighten singer Annabella into bucking up her own performance, but it didn't matter. Under the name Lieutenant Lush, George did a couple of shows, including the one at the Rainbow, singing one number with the group, and was duly noticed. The music press wrote about him. Ashley Goodall of EMI records offered him a solo deal. George preferred to bide his time, and other work was coming in.

A friend, Mad Jean, got him some work styling an 'authentic punk look' for a Royal Shakespeare Company production of

Naked Robots. He persuaded Peter Small of Street Theatre, a clothes shop off Carnaby Street, to provide free costumes in return for a mention in the programme. Small was impressed by George's talents as a stylist and soon employed him as a window-dresser. Small was then further impressed with the clothing ideas George concocted with young designer Sue Clowes, impressed enough to set them up in their own shop round the corner. They named it the Foundry.

George was still dead keen on forming a group. He'd turned down EMI's offer because he feared they'd treat him like a pro-duct and try and mould him into something he wasn't. George could do his own moulding, thank you very much. But when Mikey Craig wandered up to him one night as he was DJing in Planets and said, 'Would you like to get a band together?', George's ears pricked up.

MIKEY

Forty-one floors over Tokyo, in the Imperial Suite of the Keio Plaza hotel, Culture Club's end-of-tour party is winding down to a gentle close. It was a subdued affair even at its height, when the group were presented with gold discs for 'great sales' of *Colour By Numbers*, and now, around midnight, everyone is drifting off to bed. Mikey disappeared ages ago, George has just gone, Roy and Alison are just about to follow. Jon, unusually, will have a drink or two in the bar before retiring.

Suddenly Mikey bounds back into the room. After a quick change, he's now clad rather fetchingly in a black string vest, impenetrably dark shades, black-and-white striped shorts and a billowing raincoat. 'Just thought I'd check out a couple of these clubs,' he announces, beaming, then whisks out again.

Much later that same night and by now considerably the worse for wear, I arrive at Tokyo Club. A small night spot in the chic district of Harajuku, it's a home from home for all the Western fashion designers and models who work in Tokyo. And there, centre stage, taking all the attention, is Mikey Craig dancing, somewhat lasciviously, on a table with a blonde model.

Some people would say Mikey is slow and lazy. Others would describe him as 'laid back'. I'll just say he strikes me as a cool customer and leave it at that. But whatever you call it, his temperament is very different from George's or Jon's. Jon has described himself as 'a bit of a puritan'. Mikey is nothing of the sort. He enjoys his worldly pleasures, he still likes going out on the razzle long after the others have given it up and he looks forward to a time when Culture Club won't be so all-consuming and he'll be able to spend more time 'just . . . living'. He is not always prepared to put up with the routine hard work of being a pop star, especially not when it seems that George is creaming off all the credit and publicity. Mikey finds that much harder to cope with than Jon or Roy. So George gets annoyed with Mikey and Mikey gets annoyed with George and at times it leads to real problems within the group.

Mikey is wary of strangers at first. Journalists especially, he usually leaves to George. It took me a while to feel that I knew him even a little. But once I had narrowed the distance a bit, I discovered a friendly and gentle bloke.

Michael Emile Craig was born on 15 February 1960, in Hammersmith, London – just half a mile from the Odeon, where the *Kiss Across The Ocean* video was recorded. He has four brothers and two sisters and his family were 'working class, definitely, but the rules and morals of the family were kind of middle class. You know, we had to have good manners and so on and so forth.'

At the age of five, Mikey was completely crazy about the Monkees. 'I had every record they ever released. My father used to take me to Woolworths every weekend to buy Monkees records.' But Mikey's parents weren't going to encourage him to go into music. His father had been a singer with various Jamaican bands before coming to Britain to fight in the war. Having given up music to become a milling engineer, he knew how hard it was to make it and was dead set on his children joining secure, respectable professions.

But at school, Mikey found it hard to conjure up much enthusiasm for academic work. Only English caught his imagination, and that only because of a charismatic teacher called Dr Valentine. When he left, Mikey lost interest. Nor did he make many lasting friends. Apart from himself, there were only three or four other blacks there. 'You had to be more or less white yourself. The friends I had at school were just fair-weather friends.' He was good enough at football to play for both the school and the borough and to be invited to do trials for Fulham and Brentford Football Clubs. His parents wouldn't hear of it, though. They still wanted him to be a lawyer or a doctor.

Mikey was full grown by the age of thirteen and began to 'scamper about and go to pubs and things'. He began hanging around in Soho discos and got to be a pretty good dancer. 'I used to dance a hell of a lot and I was far better than I am now.'

Often Mikey used to walk past a large white Georgian house, just down the road from his parents' place. 'Every time I passed it I looked at it,' he remembers. He was about fifteen at the time. A friend rang him up one day to say he'd been thrown out of his house and was now staying with Erin Pizzey, the writer and organizer of homes for battered women. Why didn't Mikey come round? It turned out that Erin Pizzey's house was the same one Mikey had been staring at all the time. Erin's daughter Cleo became Mikey's girlfriend.

By this time Mikey had graduated from the dance floor to the DJ booth, spinning funk and 100 mph gay disco at a place called Club Sept in Soho. He soon discovered he'd really rather be playing an instrument instead. A friend lent him a bass guitar 'under mysterious circumstances' and he began to teach himself bass-lines from Bob Marley records. The friend eventually took it back again, and Mikey bought his own bass.

He and Cleo were living in a flat and had their first child, Kito. Mikey took on a succession of labouring jobs before securing a position as a tape operator in a recording studio. Six months after the birth of their second child, Amber, Cleo decided to move to Bristol where her mother had another house. Mikey followed and soon began playing bass in a number of Bristol bands. It was better than working in a studio but it wasn't very satisfying. Frustrated by the lack of opportunity and keen to form a band of his own, he persuaded Cleo to come back to London.

A few months later, sitting round in the flat in Erin Pizzey's house where he and Cleo now lived, he noticed a story in the *NME*. There was a picture of George and Annabella from Bow Wow Wow. Mikey was intrigued: the story suggested that Malcolm McLaren was thinking of forming a band for George.

Mikey rang an acquaintance who worked for McLaren at World's End. McLaren didn't seem to have special plans for George after all, so Mikey arranged to be introduced to the singer.

JON

·

On a bullet train sliding out through the red- and blue-roofed Tokyo suburbs, Jon Moss is telling me about this new song Culture Club have just written called, he says, 'War is Stupid'. The idea of making a statement seems to please him.

'It's like a chant. You're debasing it into a childish, stupid thing that men do, which is basically what war is.' Jon dismisses Frankie Goes To Hollywood's 'Two Tribes' – climbing the charts back in Britain as we speak – as too sensationalist. 'We don't get cheap laughs out of issues.'

Further down the carriage, in an interview with the British pop programme, *The Tube*, George is making a statement about another issue. 'Keep the GLC,' he tells the cameras, a reference to the popular campaign against the Conservative government's plans to abolish London's elected council.

I don't register this immediately but Jon must have had one

ear on the interview all the time because suddenly he leaps up and shouts over angrily: 'Don't bloody say that!'

Before anyone knows what's really happening, George and Jon are running at each other down the aisle in a full-tilt, fist-waving row. George wins on points – 'I'll say what I like!' – but Jon, though God knows if he's really that calculating, has effectively stifled an opinion he doesn't agree with. *The Tube* can't use the clip.

Conservative both by temperament and by conviction, Jon Moss is more than Culture Club's drummer. He's also, in Roy Hay's words, 'sort of part manager of the band'. Articulate, intelligent and possessed of oceans of charm, he's a friendly and likeable person who remains level-headed in a crisis but is capable of unleashing a fiery temper when it suits him. Off duty, he wears Italian suits, drives a BMW and seems more like a successful young businessman than an internationally famous pop star. He is, of course, both. With Jon you can never escape the feeling that he's ultimately not that interested in fame or pop music or even money. Everything seems to be a means to an end. He is a hard bargainer. I would hate to work for Jon Moss.

He was born on 11 September 1957, the illegitimate son of a Jewish girl from Middlesbrough living in London and a professional violinist. He ferreted out these details himself in his mid-teens and wonders whether his interest in music was inherited from his father. He was adopted by the Moss family, because his mother was unable to look after him, and christened Jonathan Aubrey.

The Moss family were very wealthy. Grandfather Moss, one of thirteen children, had worked in a Brighton pawnbroker's and slept every night on a bench in the back. Each morning he toured the hotels of the town collecting the platinum filaments from broken lightbulbs. Incredibly, after a year or so, he had enough platinum to set himself up in business. He imported binoculars, was the first person to introduce the zipper boot into the country and eventually opened a menswear shop.

Jon's foster-father, Lionel Moss, began by cleaning his

father's shop windows and ended up expanding that one shop into the Alkit chain of forty-eight. He made a fortune that's rumoured to be even bigger than Jon's and went into tax exile in Monaco a few years ago. 'Business,' comments Jon, who certainly learnt from him, 'is what he was made for.'

Jon had a 'happy and secure' unorthodox Jewish childhood in the wealthy London district of Hampstead. He went to local public schools, was a keen enough boxer to be encouraged to go professional but didn't often have to fight himself out of trouble. He found he could usually charm his way out instead.

Though he cared little for school, he stayed on to do A-levels but didn't want to go to university. 'All my friends who had gone to university had turned into ponces.' He lasted six weeks as a buyer in his father's business before deciding that the rag trade wasn't for him either. Music was where he wanted to make his way. As a young child he used to pick out pop tunes on the family piano. At the age of thirteen, he began bashing about on his elder brother David's drum kit. With the boy from over the road, Nick Feldman – a lifelong friend who's now, as Nick de Sprig, in the group Wang Chung – he formed a band called Pig William and persuaded the school to let them put on a couple of concerts. After school, Pig William became Phone Bone Boulevard, then Pastrami Barmy, then Eskimo Norbert, a group whose only recorded achievement was being booed off while supporting Thomas Dolby at a St Paul's school concert. 'We made a few demos, had a few dodgy managers, all that rubbish.'

Jon also auditioned for 'lots of really horrible groups', but was usually shown the door as soon as they spied his unfashionably non-flared trousers and puny drum kit.

'It might be hard now to get into a band, but before punk it was impossible,' he remembers. 'There was no way in. All the 1960s musicians had grown up and formed a fortress that was impenetrable for young musicians . . . unless you were a genius.'

Which Jon wasn't. He looked for other ways to tackle the problem. After 300 letters and a lot of white lies, he landed a tape operator's job at the Marquee studios. It wasn't much. Jon had to call the producers 'sir' and earned the princely sum of £16 for a sixty-hour week. 'The music business before punk,' Jon reflects, 'was Victorian.' One day the owner hit him – 'I think I'd said something wrong in front of a client' – and Jon walked out.

He worked here and there. Three months in a printing firm. A month selling cakes for a friend. Or trying to. With long scraggy hair and a beaten-up old red ski jacket, Jon would wander into a shop, pull a cake out of an old brown paper bag and say: 'What about one of these, then?' It was a spectacularly unsuccessful selling technique. Jon didn't sell a single cake. He then worked as a van driver for his father while doing a bit of 'wheeler dealing' on the side. The van was useful for carting his drums around and also, after dark, for 'other . . . purposes – you know, living at home and everything'.

(I don't know if this is now a side of himself Jon would prefer to have glossed over, but I once quoted that last bit in a *Smash Hits* article and later got a severe ticking off from an angry George for making one of 'his' band seem 'laddish'. Jon wasn't too chuffed about it either.)

Desperate to get back into 'the business', Jon landed a job at the Good Earth agency run by Bob England, now boss of Towerbell Records, and Paul King, these days manager of Tears For Fears. It was 'really boring'. He'd spend all day ringing up universities trying to persuade 'all these arrogant tossers in student unions who knew nothing about music' to book 'all these pretty naff bands' the agency handled. One night they all went to see this new group called Darts and the next day Jon was unemployed again. Bob England had gone off to manage them and closed the agency down.

Meanwhile, punk had erupted. Jon, a 'long-haired hippy into "real" music', had seen the Sex Pistols and dismissed them as 'rubbish'. 'Then one day the penny dropped. Something was happening and you could really feel it.' Keen to get in on the act, Jon answered a likely 'drummer wanted' ad and was summoned into the presence of 'all these really filthy guys with really short hair and really odd clothes . . . but there was something exciting about it'. It was the Clash, then on the verge of signing with CBS, but their identity was meant to be a secret.

'I said, "You're the Clash, aren't you?" and Joe Strummer went, "How do *you* know?" I said, "Well, it's written on the back of your jacket!"'

He got the audition, got all his hair cut off and promptly got beaten up by the jealous ex of his then girlfriend. Things with Clash didn't work out either. 'They were always promising things but nothing ever happened.' Jon argued all the time with guitarist Mick Jones ('he was a schmuck') and manager Bernie Rhodes. The Clash saw themselves as a gang of revolutionaries; Jon, then as now, was well to the right. Two months after the audition he rang Bernie Rhodes and said: 'Look, it's not me. I don't believe all this political shit and I don't believe you believe it.' Exit, pursued by threats.

With a friend called Riff Regan he formed a punk band called London. They did all the right things – jumped up and down, spat, sang angry words and swore at their audiences – and promptly came to the attention of Simon Napier-Bell, now manager of Wham! Having managed the Yardbirds and John's Children in the 1960s, Napier-Bell was completely out of touch after several years abroad. It was only after signing London that he realized that *every* band of the day was jumping up and down, spitting, singing angry songs and swearing at their audiences.

'They seemed like the nastiest, roughest, most working-class group ever,' Napier-Bell recalls. 'They used to come in the office and spit all over the place. Jon was the worst of the lot.'

Napier-Bell was therefore somewhat taken aback when he had to ring Jon at his parents' house one day and the extremely well-spoken Mrs Moss answered the phone. 'It wasn't much fun managing them because they played the part *far* too well.' Still, for a while, it worked. They toured with the Stranglers, released a single, 'Everyone's A Winner', and watched it edge its way into the bottom of the charts.

'It was the greatest period of my life,' enthuses Jon. 'I'd done it. Touring with one of the biggest groups, having a record that was *actually played on the radio*. It was like WOW! A brilliant feeling.'

Of course, it didn't last. London quickly split up and Jon replaced the departing Rat Scabies in Damned for a spell of touring, fighting and 'beer on the head'. Jon affects distaste at the memory – 'It wasn't really me' – but at the time seems to have really enjoyed all the drugs, drink and action. He must also have still been playing up the prole bit, because Captain Sensible later recalled his surprise on turning up at Jon's house one afternoon and having 'a butler' answer the door.

On New Year's Eve 1977, driving to see the Ramones with 'punk comedian' Johnny Rubbish, Jon had a bad car crash. After 300 stitches – leaving him with the scar on his right cheek – and ten days in hospital with not one of the Damned coming to visit him, he decided to leave that band too.

Guitarist Lu was the one Damned member Jon had really got on well with. Lu had hand-built a studio at his mother's house in Norfolk and he and Jon repaired there to write 'all these really manic, dark songs – we wrote enough for about three albums in four weeks'. Back in London, they recruited a band and found rehearsal space in a derelict mansion owned by a 'mad dentist' Jon knew and populated by a lot of Jon's biker friends. He was on the dole, still doing his 'wheeler-dealing' and having the time of his life.

'The Edge were a bloody good band, really manic and powerful. Lu was a genius but a bit of a cunt, very difficult to work with. Not dissimilar to George. I'm more of an organizer and I always tend to pick up with people like that.'

The rot started to set in when The Edge discovered they could make pots of money doing session work. They became the Belvederes, backing band for one Jane Aire and Jon did 'a really stupid thing'. He had an affair with Ms Aire while still living with his girlfriend. The band split up, he had to leave his girlfriend and move out of his flat. He had nothing left.

For three months he sat and stared at his bedroom wall. His father tried to encourage him to give up music and he toyed with ideas. One day he'd announce he wanted to be a gemologist, the next day a farmer.

'All I wanted to do was music. If I couldn't do that I didn't want to do anything. I couldn't even be bothered to kill myself. Every morning I got out of bed, and then it started . . .'

In the end, a weekend Exegesis course got him out of it. Jon is ambivalent about it now, but it certainly seems to have had some effect on him. He followed it up with a 'wonderful' three-week relationship, a spell of playing with a group called the Nips, his brief liaison with Adam Ant, and a new job in a video company.

Although Jon had been to hell and back over the last seven years, he'd been learning and growing steadily more ambitious as he went along. What he wanted more than anything was a band in which he could be more than just the drummer. When George, having got his phone number from mutual friend Kirk Brandon, rang and invited him to an audition, Jon was already – again in Roy's words – 'the old pro', looking for a break.

ROY

'**R**oy ... *Roy!*' George calls across the table, demanding the guitarist's attention. 'Roy, tell Dave about that conversation you had with your dad – you know, the one about petrol.'

September 1983, a small restaurant somewhere in Munich and things are getting a bit hysterical. Jon's trying to sell Roy a car, George is loudly and eagerly seizing any opening for creative bitchiness, everyone's quaffing outsize steins of German beer, tucking into positively monstrous portions of *schweinefleisch*, picking at almost surrealistically huge prawn cocktails and giggling fit to bust at endless jokes cracked at the expense of the bemused German record company people who are sitting quietly at the end of the table waiting to pick up the tab for it all. At this moment, Culture Club seem like the friendliest and funniest pop group I've ever met.

So, Roy's conversation with his father, a retired clerk:

DAD (*reading the paper, disgruntled*): Petrol's going up.

ROY (*dismissively*): Who *cares*?

DAD (*rocking with pleasure*): It's *good* to hear a son of mine say that!

Born in Southend on 12 August 1961 and a resident of various parts of Essex just about ever since, Roy is very much the suburban boy made good. His chief pleasures in life seem, not unreasonably, to be the time-honoured twin pastimes of making money and spending it. His 1960s mock-Tudor mansion in Essex – 'It's not like, er, a footballer's house, you know,' he'll say defensively – has chandeliers, a swimmingpool, a small recording studio in 'the grounds', a 'fantastic stereo with millions of compact discs because I love 'em', an office that is 'completely covered with synthesizers and things' and contains at least three home computers. There's a Jaguar and a Golf and maybe a couple of other things parked in the garage. In Tokyo, Roy's wife Alison seemed to go out shopping for clothes every single day so God knows what kind of wardrobe the pair of them have. Roy also seems always to be buying cameras and watches and everything.

He is very proud of it all.

With his white leather jackets and shades and custom-built funny-shaped silver guitars and all that, Roy is in one sense the closest thing to the conventional idea of a rock star that Culture Club have. On the other hand, he's quiet and giggly and not in the least bit arrogant. He takes his work seriously and, despite a couple of notable occasions where he publicly dissented from group decisions, tends to swim with the tide.

From Southend, his family moved to Canvey, then to Corringham, near Basildon, where they've lived ever since. Depeche Mode, Alison Moyet and Helen Terry also come from this part of the world. His father worked as a clerk in the docks and the Hay family ('a sort of respectable family') lived in 'a nice little bungalow'. Roy's mother gave him the middle name Ernest and he's been trying to live it down ever since.

He was educated at local comprehensive schools and distinguished himself neither in classroom nor on the playing field. From the age of eight his parents had him take piano lessons. At fifteen he rebelled and took up the guitar instead. For the next couple of years he was the kind of kid who painstakingly learnt all the latest Led Zeppelin riffs and spent his entire time trying to prove he was better at playing them than all the other guitarists in the neighbourhood.

He left school at sixteen and drifted into a job with a London insurance firm. It took him three years to get bored enough with that to find another job. 'A friend of mine was a hairdresser and I thought, well, he seems to be having a good time.' So Roy tried it too. It was a bit galling at first, 19-year-old Roy having to take lessons from a 16-year-old girl at this small salon in Stamford, Essex. But once over that hump, he began to enjoy himself.

All the while, he'd kept playing. He switched back and forth between piano and guitar, playing in bedroom bands with friends and often making 'little demo tapes' at home. 'I'd sit there going from one tape recorder to another, you know, and borrow a drum kit occasionally and put down a beat. You build up a picture. You start to find out what songs and music are about.'

In June 1981 at Croc's nightclub in Rayleigh, Essex he met Miss Right in the shape of Alison Green. He also met Alison's brother, Robin, who had a band called Russian Bouquet. Roy became their guitarist. Meanwhile, a friend from the insurance office, one Keith Giddons, was in the habit of popping into the Street Theatre shop where George was then working. George had mentioned he was looking for a guitarist and, well, Keith mentioned that he happened to know one.

That's all there was to it.

BRITAIN

March 1981. Adam Ant was lodged at the top of the UK album charts and Roxy Music were having their first ever number one single with 'Jealous Guy', a tribute to the recently deceased John Lennon. In Britain, a group of breakaway Labour MPs were forming the Social Democratic Party and in the USA John Hinckley Jr, the 25-year-old son of a Denver oil tycoon, was trying to assassinate Ronald Reagan outside the Washington Hilton. Helen Terry was working on stories for a series of 'non-sexist, non-racist' children's books and the Wham! boys, George Michael and Andrew Ridgeley, were in the middle of their second-last term at Bushey Meads school. After ten years of slogging around America, REO Speedwagon were topping all charts while, back in Britain, a new Birmingham group called Duran Duran were watching their first-ever release, 'Planet Earth', clamber to number twelve in the charts.

And Jon Moss was meeting George O'Dowd for the first time.

Things were already moving. After their meeting at Planets,

George and Mikey had teamed up. George wasn't sure just how much he could accomplish with only a bass player, but what the hell? He'd turned down the EMI deal because he felt vulnerable and uncertain without the security of a musically competent band behind him, and this was as good a place to start one as any. The pair recruited a guitarist called Suede, George came up with the name Sex Gang Children and the three of them even wrote a song or two together, with George nicking some lyrics from his friend Myra's poetry book. But nothing really began to gel until Jon came along.

George had a boyfriend called Kirk Brandon. A broody, earnest sort of character, Kirk seemed to model himself on James Dean and even had his own group. It was called Theatre Of Hate, one of the better of the doomy, post-punk groups, and George was their biggest fan. He used to go to all their shows, help manager Terry Razor set up their equipment and would proudly point out Kirk to any passing friend. Ever since George had started talking about being a singer, Kirk had encouraged him. And when George and Mikey were stuck for a drummer, Kirk put them in touch with Jon Moss, an acquaintance since the time Kirk's group had played a concert before the assembled hell's angels at The Edge's mansion.

Jon had done his bit with Adam. He'd turned down a job with the Ramones. A notable exception to the tired rule that all drummers are slow, boring and thick, he was still looking for a situation where he could contribute beyond simply sitting at the back and banging away. Startled by George's thirteen-to-the-dozen telephone manner when the phone call came, but intrigued when George jabbered that he'd been kicked out of Bow Wow Wow for being too effeminate, Jon eventually managed to get an address out of him. He loaded up his drums and hauled them down to a place near the Elephant and Castle.

For Jon this was just another audition. Until he met George. 'I remember thinking, "What an odd guy – he looks like a clown",' Jon says. 'There was something very attractive about him. Very sexy. I was amazed that I actually found a *man* sexy. Except he wasn't a man. He was like a . . . thing.'

The other two seemed all right too, though Jon quickly got pissed off with Mikey bumming cigarettes off him all the time. They played. He thought their two songs were 'horrible' and wasn't overly impressed with their musicianship either. But he liked George's voice straight away and was pleased that they encouraged him to play something more interesting than a standard backbeat. When he went home that night, he left his drumkit behind. George was overjoyed. It meant Jon, whom he considered 'a bit naff but awfully pretty', would be coming back again.

In almost every respect, George and Jon were perfect opposites. Jon's background was wealthy Hampstead Jewish; George's Irish Catholic working-class. Jon was always a bit of a tearaway, but essentially conservative. He took his punishment at school and would later argue in favour of school uniforms. George was an anarchic, argumentative personality who refused the cane the same way he refused any uniform but his own and, indeed, any shit from anyone at all. Jon was analytical; George intuitive. Jon was a bit of a lad; George was as camp as Christmas. And above all, George was the walking, talking, made-up, dressed-up living embodiment of London's underground nightlife. Jon thought the whole scene stank.

'Smear stuff on your face; tacky, dirty, everything falls apart. Nice exterior, very dressy, but underneath it's dirty. There was no spirit, no faith, no religion. Ungodly. The Blitz thing was like walking into Hell, it was like Berlin in the 1930s. When I go to Hell, that's what I expect it to be like,' he told *The Face* in August 1982.

Complete opposites, but they each found in the other something that was lacking in themselves.

George: 'I got on very well with Mikey but he's not a good influence on me 'cause he's very slow and lazy. I need someone to say, "Right, do this, do that and let's get on with it." And when I met Jon that's what happened really.'

Jon: 'I wanted to meet somebody that was talented, not someone who made up for their lack of talent with sloganeering. And in George I found that. The great thing about George when we started – shame he's not like that any more – is that he actually listened to what I was saying.'

What Jon said first was that they'd never get anywhere with a name like Sex Gang Children.

'You wanker! Shortarse! What do you know about it?' is how Jon remembers George's reply.

'Look, man,' argued Jon, believing that the name conjured up

49

all that was dark, ugly and decadent about the Blitz scene. 'We need religion, we need warmth, we need colour. People don't want to know about getting pissed and falling on the floor. They want a reason. They want to believe in something. They want faith. They want to work.'

Eight years of failure and false starts had left this particular puritan with a renewed faith in the work ethic and the urge to be in a band that sold millions of records. He didn't want to write songs for the London trendies he so despised. He felt he had nothing to prove to his peers. He wanted to write songs for mothers and little sisters and next door neighbours. So Sex Gang Children had to go.

George went away and thought about it. At the time his ambition was still to be the most outrageous person in London. The idea of being a lovable, international pop star was a new one. He gave in and came up with the name Caravan Club. Which got changed to Can't Wait Club. Which ended up as Culture Club.

Another group took over the name Sex Gang Children. No one has heard of them since.

Jon also said that Suede wasn't good enough, something that George wasn't musically experienced enough to notice and Mikey wasn't confident enough to say. This opinion was confirmed after they'd written a couple of songs – 'Eyes Of Medusa' and 'I'm An Animal' – and demo'd them courtesy of the still interested Ashley Goodall at EMI. A friend who's heard it tells me this tape is 'Bow Wow Wow-ish' and quite good, but Culture Club weren't too pleased with it and neither were EMI. They were least pleased with Suede's playing and so the guy got the sack.

They auditioned loads of guitarists that Jon knew, but none of them seemed to fit. 'They just had the wrong attitude,' says George. 'We wanted someone that would come along and be a bit naïve about it all and would just play what we wanted and get into the ideas.' Then Roy came along and did just that. The others weren't that impressed with his playing, but they liked the fact that he was enthusiastic, open to suggestions and completely unruffled by the appearance either of Mikey (then going through a weird phase with plaits and a mohican and everything) or George (his usual self). George particularly liked him because he seemed a real ordinary suburban Joe and nothing at all to do with the nightclub crowd he was now trying to transcend. In fact, with

Alison Green and her brother Robin, Roy had actually explored London nightlife a lot more than any of them knew, but he kept it to himself. Roy was in.

With Jon at the helm, the group began to organize itself. George and Jon began ferreting out all their respective contacts and started working with Sue Clowes on ideas for a 'look'. All four got to work on writing songs. At first Jon worked with George a lot, taking his raw ideas and suggesting ways of structuring them. But soon it settled down into a process that involved Jon and Mikey coming up with rhythmic ideas, George contributing melodies and lyrics, Roy working out arrangements and chord structures and all of them arguing, shouting, swearing and throwing things at each other all the time.

It wasn't easy going. Roy would travel into town on the train three nights a week right after finishing work at the hairdresser's, rehearse for three hours, then travel back to Essex again, rarely getting to bed before the small hours. Mikey, with a wife and two kids at home, seemed to find it all particularly difficult. The others remembers him always being late and never having enough money to pay for his share of rehearsal space. And then there were the arguments. Always arguments.

By October 1981 they were ready to play their first concert, and did so at Roy's local club: Croc's in Rayleigh, Essex. This had been the venue for many a punk group in the late 1970s and had become famous during the new romantic days as the home ground of electronic foursome, Depeche Mode. Culture Club, then very raw and raucous with just three instruments cranked up painfully loud, went down a storm. They played, in embryonic form, most of the material that would end up on their first album and were invited back to play on Boxing Day.

Mikey remembers the audience: 'The age group there is about sixteen to twenty-two and everybody goes out of their way to overdress and get pissed on a Saturday night. You'd find a bunch of rockabillies, a bunch of skinheads probably, a bunch of new romantics and Kid Creole lookalikes, all in the same place, which was really interesting.'

And very much a sign of the times.

On Valentine's Day, 1981, Steve Strange and Rusty Egan moved out of the Blitz to host a much larger one-off event at London's Rainbow Theatre. Dubbed the People's Palace, it was the Blitz crowd's coming-out ball, a sort of new romantic Woodstock. Ultravox, then at number two with the monumentally dull 'Vienna', played on stage but nobody really cared. The real spectacle was elsewhere. In the corridors and bars of the theatre, scores of photographers, professional and amateur, snapped urgently away at a passing peacock throng that was only too willing to oblige with a pose and a pout. In the foyer, photographer Richard Young had actually set up a booth and a white backdrop, all the better to snap them with. The only thing missing was a conveyor belt.

It wasn't a concert. Still less a party. As the media went about ensuring that it wouldn't miss out this time, it was more like a shooting gallery. And for a crowd whose main aim in life had always been dressing up and getting their pictures in the papers as often as possible, that meant it was the closest thing to heaven.

If the new romantics ever had a *perfect moment*, then that – FLASH! – was it. From then on the whole scene began to dissipate.

In refusing to be pinned down to any one particular style or sound, new romantic successfully avoided being marketable and thus also avoided becoming the Next Big Thing. It didn't turn into a new centre, but it eroded enough of the old one – challenging traditional rock patterns of consumption at least to the extent of shifting attention from live concerts to club life, from weighty LPs to dance-mix 12-inch singles – to leave everyone wondering just what was going on. Once it was clear that the toy soldier look – the frilly shirts and velvet breeches usually associated with the term new romantic – was definitely not hip, nor even saleable in the high street, it was suddenly very hard to work out what was.

Into the uncertain vacuum roared a confusion of sounds and styles. There was a new fad or revival every week. Rockabilly, most notably in the shape of the Stray Cats, enjoyed a brief renaissance while Shakin' Stevens, an old rocker who'd been ploughing round pubs and clubs for years, suddenly found fame and fortune. Other fractional revivals, usually based round one group, one London club night and one budding McLaren, were less lucky. Brief revisits of psychedelia, be-bop and beatnik all failed to stick. As people cast round for the right new sound, anything became grist to the pop mill. Jazz, Latin, northern soul, funk, Euro-disco, African, Indian and Chinese musics were all variously used as ethnic spice to enliven the staples of mainstream pop. In the case of African music, for example, this boiled down to little more than Adam and Bow Wow Wow basing their sound round the drums of Burundi. But it all added to the confusion of a restless, rowdy, eclectic and ultimately brilliant year for white pop music. In 1981 there seemed to be only one rule: don't stand still.

But people were still looking for a Next Big Thing. What would it be? Virgin Records must have thought they had the answer when they signed Blue Rondo A La Turk for a reportedly absurd amount of money. This band, who'd grown out of the same club crowd as Spandau Ballet, looked like a sure bet. They had their own supposedly hip sound: a mix of Latin and disco. They had their own supposedly hip look: 1940s zoot suits and scrambled-egg ties. They had an ideology, based round the idea of the anti-austerity zoot suit as the very first expression of youth adversity through clothes, to go with it. And they had an unholy amount of gushing publicity before anyone had even heard them play.

They had all this. They bombed completely. What could a poor record company do?

The more precarious end of the fashion industry found it all hard to cope with too. Once the short-lived frilly shirt boom was over, small clothes manufacturing businesses, the sweat shops all over London's East End, began to go to the wall. By the end of the year, hundreds had gone out of business. They had no idea any more how to predict what people wanted to wear.

What was happening was a complete dissolution of the traditional British relationship between music, style and subculture. Youth consensus? Not any longer. At one time, youth factions as diverse as those Mikey spotted at Croc's that night would have been at each other's throats. But style was now no longer a badge of allegiance. It was simply this week's outfit. Something to wear for a night out but hardly something worth

53

getting into a fight over. Fashion, and pop music along with it, seemed suddenly to have lost its old importance. Fragments reigned.

No more subculture, more a culture club.

And if the point needed to be pressed home, there were the latter-day punks, an exception to prove the rule, furiously clinging on to an idealized spirit of 1976. The 'Punk's Not Dead' movement of awful Oi bands like the Exploited or the 4-Skins still used 'anarchy' as their watchword. But there was nothing anarchic about the way they clung ever more tightly to the totems of a rigid form. Far from it. Punk actually now seemed to express a deep desire for order amid a subcultural chaos the participants had ceased to understand. A lot of people labelled the movement 'fascist'. Particularly after a busload of skinheads arriving in Southall, a predominantly Asian area of London, for a 4-Skins concert at the Hamborough Tavern, provoked a race riot that left the venue a burnt-out ruin and a lot of questions hanging over what punk had let itself become.

While the punks still tried to shout 'anarchy' from the roof-tops, everyone else was dancing in the ruins. One of the year's more important fads was Brit-funk. Initially used to describe bands like Linx, Light Of The World, Level 42 and others who played a home-grown version of American jazz-funk and marketed it like pop, it broadened out to become an umbrella term for any band, black or white, that made even remotely funky music. Tagged, as it was, to anything with a dancefloor beat, the adjective 'funky' became ever more meaningless. This concern with the exigencies of the dance floor did, however, mark the seeds of a new mainstream beginning to solidify beneath the bubbling stylistic chaos.

The new romantics had always asserted a soul boy history and a continuity with disco culture. After their first couple of hits, Spandau Ballet ditched numb Euro-disco electronics, which they'd never been very good at anyway, and set about trying to make a funk record. The result, recorded with the horn section of Brit-funk band Beggar & Co, was 'Chant Number One'. It became their biggest hit. Duran Duran, the only other important and lasting group to grow directly out of new romantic culture, were similarly involved in trying to develop a British form of disco. By the end of the year, all sorts of people were mining the same seam: Heaven 17, ABC, Haircut One Hundred. And in turn, disco itself was being prised apart and restructured by people like Grace Jones, Kid Creole and the Tom Tom Club.

Meanwhile, the old New Wave seemed to be petering out. Blondie had their last big hit with 'Rapture'. The original Specials had their last big hit with one of the records of the year, 'Ghost Town', a song that eerily captured the mood of a nation torn by an unprecedented wave of uprising, riots, looting and fighting in the street. The Jam and the Police both had a largely indifferent year.

On the other hand, there were lots of one, two and three-hit wonders. Incredible though it now seems, The Teardrop Explodes, a Liverpool group led by psychedelia-fixated Julian Cope, briefly turned into a full-blown teenage sensation complete with hordes of swooning fans. Altered Images, Toyah, Kim Wilde and Hazel O'Connor also had their moments. But the two biggest sensations were Adam, who had a truly spectacular year, and the Human League. The latter began in 1981 after a split between the four founding members, with the two remaining – Philip Oakey and Adrian Wright – being largely written off as a likely failure. One year, four big hits and an album that became part of the basic 1980s record collection later, and they seemed like the biggest band in Britain. Out of all the frantic eclecticism, here was a group that finally refined a method that they and others (Soft Cell, Depeche Mode) had been working on for ages: they used modern-sounding electronic instruments to play good old-fashioned pop songs. The Human League were pushy, argumentative and almost unbearably arrogant. They were also in control and in the charts.

The New Pop had finally established itself.

The former other half of the Human League, Ian Craig Marsh and Martyn Ware, did something different. They didn't form a new group, they formed a company, the British Electronic Foundation, which included a group, Heaven 17, as part of its operation. 'We realize that it must seem to outsiders like some daft game we're playing,' Martyn Ware told me in September 1981, but it did seem to make sense: a step beyond independence or licensing deals in the practicality stakes. Heaven 17 started doing photo sessions in pinstripe executive suits, ties and briefcases. Corporate chic was in. Ex-Buzzcock Peter Shelley appeared on an LP sleeve with a suit, computer and boardroom table. Scritti Politti, then trying to break out of the independent ghetto, dressed up all their releases in packaging ripped off from Dunhill or Dior. Loads of groups included on their sleeves a legend such as 'London – Paris – New York'.

In part a joke, this in some way reflected the hard-nosed business attitude bands were adopting. Spandau Ballet, for example, had formed their own label and publishing company before they went anywhere near a major label. In their design they aimed for a muted corporate identity that stretched across all their releases. A Spandau record always looked like a Spandau record. A clutch of related releases actually looked like a product range. Designer Malcolm Garrett of Assorted iMaGes developed this approach further in his work for Duran Duran.

1982 began with number one hits for Human League, 1981's Eurovision winners Bucks Fizz and then Kraftwerk, a group whose influence had long been lurking behind this all: electronic pop, total control, corporate identity. If the New Pop established itself in 1981, this was the year in which it began to settle down. Spandau hit a bit of a trough but Duran Duran were growing all the time. Adam faded, but the Human League began to export their success across the Atlantic.

Until now, the serious-minded young arbiters of popular taste had always dismissed the charts, decried anyone with a clearly commercial motive and sought significance chiefly in the wilfully obscure. In 1982, that changed. Pop music was suddenly hip. As its circulation rocketed, *Smash Hits* became the trendy magazine to read, not just among its natural constituency of provincial teenagers, but also among the hipper and older metropolitan crowd. Simple pop groups like Dollar (then produced by Trevor Horn) and Bucks Fizz acquired a curious credibility. When Wham! arrived on the scene in the summer, they were greeted with open arms and wild enthusiasm by the same critics who two years later would be snarling and sniping at their every move.

A funny year, 1982. With the exception of Dexys Midnight Runners' success with scarecrow outfits and an unlikely combination of soul and folk – 'Come On Eileen' was the year's best-selling single – nothing seemed to happen that hadn't been set up in 1981. Kid Creole, who spent the whole of the previous year counting up the column inches but failing to find the requisite hits, finally broke through. ABC and Haircut One Hundred lost the funk tag and hit hard with well-crafted pop while other Brit-funk bands split up. Instead, seasoned American exponents like Shalamar, Marvin Gaye and Kool and the Gang held the field.

There weren't so many fads but there were a lot of great pop records. A spirit of determined diversity still reigned. The charts were still a culture club.

As soon as Culture Club had got going, Jon set about organizing the business of the band. He was determined to get it right this time, never again to be an employee. 'I had been really burned in the business and I knew all the pitfalls and I really didn't want to make those mistakes again,' he explains. 'So I wanted to have complete control without being silly. Like Spandau Ballet. They've got such tight control over everything they don't get anywhere, you know.'

His first argument was that everyone should be on equal terms. He'd learnt that from the Stranglers. They'd been through a lot of ups and downs together, but they split everything five ways and were able to keep it all in perspective. The others lacked Jon's experience but trusted his judgement. Culture Club agreed to split all proceeds four ways, no matter what. Even if, for example, a song had been written by only two of them, the money would go to all four.

The second thing he did was think about delegating. They needed to find a manager. 'I want a fat, balding, middle-aged, Jewish guy,' Jon decided. They found exactly that in the ample shape of Tony Gordon, formerly manager of the Angelic Upstarts and Sham 69. Gordon's nephew, Nick Massey, was managing Jon's old mate Nick Feldman's group, Wang Chung, so Jon approached Gordon through him. They came to a very informal relationship. No money would change hands and no contract would be signed until the group had a top ten single.

George, meanwhile, had finished working on the new Foundry

57

range: print fabric outfits covered in a cacaphony of religious symbolism that the group would later make famous. Jon had persuaded George to use the Star of David. Sue Clowes came up with a Hebrew slogan which read, 'Culture and Education, Movement of All People'. She ringed it with red roses to symbolize England. As well as the Star, with its dual Jewish and Rasta connotations, they used a Christian cross. On one shirt this had flowers next to it and aeroplanes flying over it, symbolizing its good and bad sides. The fabrics also displayed hearts and swords and flames and lots of the markings that tramps chalk on roads to notify others of a soft touch or a dangerous location. Sue Clowes had found them in a book.

George once explained the use of the symbols to me like this: 'It's like an Everyman culture where all those symbols are used together and each one contradicts the other. Used together they can't have any meaning, because they're supposed to represent different things.'

But symbols tend to have a life of their own. In autumn 1982, after Israel had invaded the Lebanon, George rang up *Smash Hits* and asked them to remove the Star of David from a photograph they were using. It had become a symbol of oppression.

Mikey, who was a little resentful he hadn't been able to contribute to the designs, was pressed into service modelling them. Soon fashion spreads on the Foundry and Culture Club began to appear in magazines like *New Sounds New Styles* and *The Face*. All the outfits were already in the Foundry shop as well as being used on stage by the time Culture Club played their second show at Croc's on Boxing Day, 1981. In the audience at that show was a keen young man from Virgin Publishing called Danny Goodwin. He was impressed. A few days later he popped into the Foundry to see George and asked him if they'd like to do a demo tape. They went in and recorded 'I'm Not Crazy' and two other songs which they later ditched, 'Put It Down' and 'Kissing To Be Clever'. Virgin were uncertain but kept in touch. So Culture Club got back in touch with Ashley Goodall at EMI and did another demo there. This time, at Tony Gordon's suggestion, they used a producer: Steve Levine, whom Gordon also now manages.

On this third demo were 'White Boy' and 'I'm Afraid Of Me'

and suddenly everything clicked. The partnership with Steve Levine, who would go on to produce their first three albums, worked out well. After experimenting with various styles, George had finally decided to try sounding like himself and for the first time was pleased with the way his voice had turned out. When they heard the tape, a lot of record companies sat up and took notice. George and Jon began going round to see them all. The big companies like Polydor and EMI seemed rude and impersonal; Island too laidback. In the end they settled on Virgin. It was small enough for everyone to know what was going on all the time, but big enough to be strong on marketing commercial pop records. Virgin also allowed Culture Club the control they wanted over the artistic side: what would be released and when, what would go on the cover and so forth. They paid for that in financial terms, though. But as Jon said at the time, wary of the myriad ways an inept company might try and market someone like George, 'I'd rather have 75 per cent of a million than 100 per cent of fuck all.' Three years later he would begin to get resentful of the amount of money Virgin were making out of the group, but at the time he was happy enough with the deal. With Steve Levine, they set about recording their first album.

From the very first, George and Jon had become really friendly. But the arguments in the group continued. 'We're all so close it's almost like having an affair,' says George. And as in an affair, the rows, even when they were so nasty that Roy ended up in tears, were usually made up and forgotten. George was always flying off the handle.

'George is very difficult to work with, you can imagine,' says Jon. 'Like, he goes, fuck off, fuck off, I don't want to, you're all wankers, and he'll walk out.'

At one point during work on the first album, George just decided he couldn't be bothered any more. As he often would in the future, he felt he had nothing at all in common with the rest of the group. Marilyn and he hatched plans to run away to the South of France and do a cabaret act with George as Sarah Bernhardt rising out of her coffin. The group was on the point of falling apart.

Then something happened that changed the whole situation.

George and Jon's relationship stopped being just like an affair. Instead, it suddenly *was* an affair. George had always fancied Jon but never really believed he was in with a chance. Now he was

59

head over heels in love and threw himself back into work with Culture Club with more enthusiasm than ever before.

They began drawing in other musicians to work with them. 'Love Twist', for example, seemed to need a toast. So they used Cleo Pizzey's younger brother Amos, a 14-year-old white rasta, and named him Captain Crucial. The connection might have persisted but Mikey and Cleo's relationship was deteriorating. All Mikey's time and money was going into the band and Cleo had had enough. She, the kids and all the Pizzey family went off to Sante Fe, New Mexico, Amos among them. These days he's back in Britain with his own band, Dark City.

Others included Phil Pickett, a keyboard player who had once had several hits with Sailor and Weasel, a toaster Mikey knew who was drafted in to do the talkover on the 12-inch version of 'Do You Really Want To Hurt Me'. For that song, one of the last they recorded for the first LP, they also decided they needed some female backing vocals. George began looking round for a singer. One night, he, Marilyn and Philip Sallon were on their way to a benefit for Andrew Logan's Alternative Miss World event at the London gay club, Heaven. It was three in the morning. Helen Terry, who had been performing at the benefit as part of Miss Binnie's Neo-Naturists – 'they used to take all their clothes off and daub themselves with body paint while I used to wear as many clothes as humanly possible and sing along, things like "Anarchy In The UK" in the style of Aretha Franklin' –was just on her way home. Marilyn pointed her out to George. 'She can sing,' he chirped. 'Go on, sing, sing,' urged George. Helen announced that she wasn't a performing poodle but did make arrangements to meet and talk about it later. She'd done session work in the past and wasn't sure about doing it again. In the end, a few days later, she did sing on the track and before long was working with the group pretty much full-time, but as an employee, not a member.

In May 1982 the first single, 'White Boy', was released. Despite a flurry of publicity, it wasn't a hit. Mikey was satisfied that the record had introduced them to the hardcore record-buying public, but George, according to Jon, 'freaked out'. He just couldn't understand why it hadn't sold. Jon said: 'Look, all you've got to do is keep releasing records until you do get a hit, it's quite logical.'

A short tour they played at the time ended with 2000 people cramming into Heaven to see Culture Club supported by Musical Youth. There was clearly enough interest for Virgin to release the next single. That was 'I'm Afraid Of Me' and that wasn't a hit either.

A lot of people in Britain were beginning to write them off. I remember round about this time the then features editor of *Smash Hits* rang me up and explained that they'd been trying to decide on a new band to cover. It was a toss-up between Culture Club and their dreadlocked competitors Haysi Fantayzee, the group formed by George's old friend Jeremy. They'd decided, he said, that Culture Club were never going to make it and he despatched me off to interview Haysi instead.

And then came 'Do You Really Want To Hurt Me'. I was in *Smash Hits* the morning the first review copies arrived. We put it on the turntable and listened, amazed. 'It sounds like Dennis Brown,' commented the editor approvingly. We played it again and again. I took a copy home and listened to it some more. I'd liked 'White Boy', was indifferent to 'I'm Afraid Of Me' but this record was clearly in a different league altogether.

A few weeks later, it got to number one.

AMERICA

Just outside the Empire State
Building, on the corner of 36th Street and Fifth Avenue, New
York City, George is coping with yet another interruption to the
brief Sunday afternoon sightseeing tour that's doubling as a
Smash Hits photo session. It's early December 1982 and this is
Culture Club's first, tentative foray into the New World. Just a
toe in the water: a long weekend comprising two shows at The
Ritz, several important business meetings and a round of interviews and photo sessions. It seems to be going well. The audience
at The Ritz last night all danced to the music and enjoyed the
English camperie – 'Are there any poufs in the audience?' 'Thank
you, girls', etc. – that George will soon be dropping from his act.
'Do You Really Want To Hurt Me' is gradually winning airplay
on all but the country-and-western stations. And Jon is finding
'dollar-orientated' Americans easy to deal with over the conference table. 'In England everybody's trying to make money but
they're ashamed to admit it. Here it's easy to talk business.'

But apart from dedicated anglophiles and those who turned

up at The Ritz – like the straight-laced, fresh-faced Canadian couple who skate up to us in Central Park and announce: 'Hi, we caught your show last night. It was *rilly* great. We're music *fanatics*! We're going to buy your record for our party next week!' – nobody yet really knows who George is. Nobody knows, but everyone notices. As we move around town, reactions are extreme. A bunch of guys in lumberjack shirts bellow obscenities at him from a passing truck. A black woman behind the counter of a souvenir shop calls over: 'I'm really jealous – your make-up is *very* good.' The turnstile operators inside the Empire State Building stare dumbfoundedly and shout: 'Hey, what are you guys? Some kind of English pop group?' The hubcap-banging operator of an exceedingly dodgy one-man band smiles delightedly as George prances about inanely on the sidewalk to his music.

And now George is getting a good-natured haranguing from an old lady. What, she wants to know, is the meaning of it all: this hat, those locks, all that make-up?

'Well,' George starts to explain, 'we're from England and –'

'I can tell you're English,' she interrupts. 'You don't have to be a mind reader to tell *that*!'

Less than a year later, George will be on the cover of *Rolling Stone*, an accolade that, in the American music business, means you've finally made it. Inside it is reported that on 16 July 1983, no fewer than eighteen singles of British origin charted in the American Top Forty, beating the previous high of fourteen on 18 June 1965. Next to George's smiling face, the cover copy reads: 'Great Britain invades America's music and style. Again.'

Back in Britain, Boy George and Culture Club were already household names. On 22 September 1982, with 'Do You Really Want To Hurt Me' at number 38 in the chart, they made their first ever appearance on Britain's most important pop show, *Top Of The Pops*. With an audience of around twelve million, a *TOTP* appearance virtually guarantees a rise up the chart, although there have been enough exceptions to this rule to keep everyone on their toes. It can make or break a record. It can make or break a group. Culture Club were therefore understandably nervous and more than usually argumentative when they went down to the BBC Television Centre in Wood Lane to record their bit. With them miming backing vocals were Helen Terry and a woman called Pat Fernandes – then earning pocket money driving George around, later to be found in the company of Wham!'s George Michael. They were even more nervous – George so much so that he couldn't keep still – when they watched the show the following night at the studio of photographer Eric Watson on a crackly little telly Virgin records sent down for this very purpose.

And all over the UK, twelve million other people watched it too.

Though the London trendies were well used to him, this was the first time most of Britain had been confronted with George in all his androgynous splendour. There was a storm in the press that took months to die down. 'Is it a boy or is it a girl?' Fleet Street cried, outraged. 'Wally of the week!' George took up an almost permanent residency in the pages of the daily papers. The record swished up the charts, a few weeks later replacing their former support act Musical Youth's 'Pass The Dutchie' in the number one slot. By Christmas, Culture Club had a second single, 'Time', and a debut LP, *Kissing To Be Clever*, both riding high in the charts. George won the *Daily Mirror*'s award for pop personality of the year. There wasn't any stopping them now.

In November 1982 at Birmingham Odeon, Culture Club played their first big concert since they'd made the chart. The fans screamed from beginning to end. It was a sign of the times. After a lull of a few years following the demise of the mid-1970s teeny groups like Slik (Midge Ure's first band) and the Bay City Rollers, screaming had come back in fashion with Gary Numan when he first hit the heights in 1979. When Adam Ant came along, his fans screamed even louder. Each New Pop group that made the grade – Duran Duran, Spandau Ballet, Haircut One Hundred, Wham!, Kajagoogoo, Paul Young – all found their new following shrieking the place down every time they appeared in public. By August 1983 it had begun to reach epidemic proportions. Duran Duran arrived back in England after recording in the Caribbean for a week of well-publicized activity. Fans mobbed them at the airport, mobbed them at their hotel. The press coined the word 'Durandemonium' to describe the reaction. It seemed like the biggest thing since Beatlemania. Duran's first stop was a benefit concert in aid of the Prince's Trust at London's Dominion Theatre before the Prince and Princess of Wales. They didn't put on a terribly good show, but the fans were too busy screaming to notice and everybody else probably too busy blocking their ears to care. The press immediately dubbed Duran 'Princess Di's favourite group'. Shortly afterwards, it was reported that when Princess Diana appeared in public, teenagers had even begun screaming at her.

1983 was a year of megastars. If Princess Diana had suddenly become a pop star, then George, Sting, Simon le Bon, Michael Jackson and the other pop personalities who thronged the daily papers were afforded a level of attention usually only granted to royalty. The New Pop was now sweeping all before it. With Spandau Ballet, Paul Young and Wham! creeping close behind and Paul Weller's Style Council maintaining a kind of loyal opposition, Culture Club and Duran Duran established an almost stifling popularity. David Bowie, the great-grandaddy of them all, swept back into the country with 'Let's Dance' and a massively successful tour. Against opposition like that, the year's touted underground trends – there was a brief fad for groups who made music by dragging large amounts of scrap metal on stage and then demolishing it all with drills and hammers – stood no chance at all. Britain was going pop crazy. The charts were all anyone cared about. Pop shows crammed the TV schedules, all the more since the arrival of the new youth-conscious Channel 4 in late 1982. The circulation of *Smash Hits* was going through the roof. And throughout it all, the screaming never stopped.

What's more, it was spreading abroad.

'I want a number one American album, that's the next thing. Duran Duran have just charted in America with "Hungry Like The Wolf" apparently, but we're number twenty-four now. They say "Do You Really Want To Hurt Me" is going to be top five and it's like selling like wild out there and it's being played all the time, but "Time" I think will be a bigger hit than "Do You Really Want To Hurt Me" because it's so American, "Time", they love it. It's sort of cruising down the highway type stuff. I mean, it was never meant to be that, you know, but I want, you know, I want fucking big hits . . .'

It's early 1983 and George is gushing.

'So the next album I wanna be like an album with the singles coming off it, 'cause that's the market we need to go for now, you know, we need to go for an album market, we need to get a number one album in America. Mind you, this album is doing fucking well there. It's sold 175,000 copies in America. Ridiculous. Sold 90,000 last week. You sell so much but you hardly go up any places, but I mean, as long as you're selling . . . We've got so many gold discs now. We've got more than Duran Duran. We *have*. We've got about fifteen. Got platinum discs for Belgium and gold ones for everywhere. Like Israel, Thailand. You know, it's ridiculous, we've got so many places now. It's great. I love it. Just clocking off somewhere every day now. Switzerland, Sweden will be number one, Australia, New Zealand, Austria, Israel. We're playing a festival in Israel, an open-air festival. They love us there because of the Star of David, they re-e-eally love us there, it's *so* outrageous. We're doing an open-air festival for 8000 people, it'll be brilliant. Amazing.'

George pauses for breath. 'There's not that many people in Israel, though, is there?'

Two years later, on 9 February 1985, at London's Grosvenor House Hotel, the British Phonographic Industry held their annual awards ceremony. For the first time ever it was a grand televised gala event, complete with a slap-up dinner, stars arriving in limos, guest celebrities all over the place – a celebration of an industry that felt confident and in the ascendant and absolutely, completely as though punk had never happened. It was a balanced evening: everyone who'd had a good year either won something or put in an appearance. Culture

Club were noticeable only by their absence. At the end of the evening, BPI chairperson and CBS managing director Maurice Oberstein took to the stage with a large, shaggy dog and made a long, fumbling speech. His delivery was haphazard and the import of his words were at first lost upon much of the company, but it soon became apparent that he was giving the Police a special award for services to the industry. They were the first British group of the post-punk period to have begun conquering markets abroad and scattering hit singles around the planet.

The Police first zipped over the Atlantic on Freddie Laker's low-budget Skytrain, carrying their instruments as hand luggage, as far back as October 1978, long before they'd had a hit anywhere. With one roadie in tow, they drove themselves up and down the East Coast for a series of small club gigs, then Lakered it back home again. Later, they had a small 1979 hit with 'Roxanne'. At the time, these efforts won them more derision than praise. Seen through the eyes of the British New Wave in the late 1970s, America was a bland land of no hope: crass, corrupting and home of some of the most awful music in the world. So strong was this view, it was held that only by sinking to *their* level was it possible to break there. Accordingly, any band that did have some American success, like the Police, was simply sneered at. Everybody knew the story of Rod Stewart.

At the same time, breaking America was what everyone – even, *especially*, the Clash who'd sung so memorably about being bored with the place – wanted to do. Not just for the money, though that was most of it, but also because if you made it in America then you'd . . . made it. Like the Beatles, you know, and the Stones. Compared to America, whose culture permeates Britain's so remorselessly, everywhere else was just a series of 'territories' to visit once in a while, do a few phone interviews with, send the odd video to and watch the royalties notch up. This didn't stop groups flogging themselves to death trying to beat a path and keep a presence around the world's more important markets, but though some favoured Japan and many were fond of Australia, America was where it really counted.

The second British Invasion of America – because that, by mid-1983, twenty-odd years after the first one, is almost certainly what it was – did not happen overnight. It took years. And it wasn't a simple matter of lots of bright new talent popping over from Britain and saying, 'here we are'. It reflected a lot of changes that were taking place in the American music industry at the time. The Police's success with 'Roxanne', for example, was initially due to Top Forty radio play. At the time, American Top Forty radio was a stodgy, hidebound laughing-stock even in the USA. But their picking up on the Police was symptomatic of a gradual loosening up on American radio. Stations that looked for a new format and began playing mostly British 'new music' (as they called it), like KROQ in Los Angeles, had a lot to do with the subsequent success of all the limey upstarts.

Dance clubs were important too. The first British records that really made people's ears prick up were things like M's 'Pop Muzik' and Gary Numan's 'Cars' – records that were crafted largely with electronic instrumentation and thus were dubbed 'electropop'. No American groups were doing anything like this. But Euro-disco-based and dance-orientated as it was, electropop was perfect fodder for American rock discos. All sorts of British records began getting played in the clubs and groups like Heaven 17, New Order, Thompson Twins, Bow Wow Wow, ABC, Ultravox, Depeche Mode, Visage and Thomas Dolby all found their American careers getting a boost from newly anglophile club DJs. In 1981, the Human League's 'Don't You Want Me' – a record that crossed the American barriers between rock, disco and pop – began breaking through in a big way. It eventually went all the way to number one. Soft Cell's 'Tainted Love', another club hit which crossed over to radio play, surged into the charts in its wake. It ended up enjoying the longest stay in the *Billboard* charts of any record ever: forty-three weeks. In early 1982, A Flock Of Seagulls, a British synthesizer group who no one gave a toss for at home, had a massive hit with 'I Ran (So Far Away)'. The wheel was now turning in America too.

British groups began going over and working the USA as hard as they could. The Thompson Twins, with a couple of dance chart hits in 'Lies' and 'In The Name Of Love' behind them, spent a lot of time there in 1982. So did Duran Duran who, up until the success of 'Hungry Like The Wolf' on its third American release, were selling more records in *Portugal* than they were in the USA. But if one thing really got the New Pop off the ground in America, it was MTV.

Music Television, to give it its full name, began cabling

music videos twenty-four hours a day on 1 August 1981. At the time, few guessed how important it would become. British bands had always spent a lot more time and care on their 'look' than had their American counterparts. This usually led to them being dismissed in the States as foppish, superficial 'fashion-plates' without a genuine rock 'n' roll idea in their heads. MTV changed all that. British groups naturally understood how to exploit the video medium long before the average, dull-looking, American rock band. Adam Ant, Eurythmics, Billy Idol, Madness, Police and even Def Leppard, a Sheffield heavy metal band whose success in the States has since been gargantuan, all used MTV for a leg up into the charts. Duran Duran's 'Hungry Like The Wolf' was a favourite on MTV fully three months before it began to get played on radio. The radio stations, to their surprise, had begun getting requests for things they weren't even playing. The world had turned upside-down.

As 1982 turned into 1983, the unlikeliest groups began to pop up in the *Billboard* charts: the Fixx, Squeeze, Talk Talk, Kim Wilde, Haircut One Hundred, Thomas Dolby, Style Council and Wang Chung all garnered a degree of success. The bigger names began breaking through as well. Adam had a hit with 'Goody Two Shoes'; Dexys Midnight Runners had a number one with 'Come On Eileen'. The Eurythmics scored with 'Sweet Dreams' and found themselves on the cover of *Rolling Stone*. The reaction to this coverage of 'dressed-up disco' was mixed. 'So one truly miserable hit single is all it takes to get on the cover of your magazine?' wrote Gene Baxter of Greenbelt, Maryland, to *Rolling Stone* after that Eurythmics cover. 'Can we expect cover stories this fall on Men Without Hats and Michael Sembello?' And that issue and the British Invasion special with George on the cover a couple of months later both sold noticeably badly. It was clear that what was happening in America was similar to what had already happened in Britain. These groups were reaching a new, younger audience that cared little for the pomp and circumstance, politics and pretension of the rock tradition. They wanted glamour and good fun, and they got it.

By mid-July 1983, no less than six of *Billboard*'s top ten singles were British, from Police, Kajagoogoo, Madness, Duran Duran, Culture Club and, a hardy survivor from the original British Invasion, the Kinks. To complete the picture, by the end

71

of the year, the USA had its own version of Britain's *Smash Hits*
to cater for the new audience: *Star Hits.*

'In America,' George asserted in New York back in December
1982, 'you can sell a record but you can't sell a look. I'd love to
break down that barrier and make people stick hats on their heads
and dreadlocks on their hair and just . . . *indulge* a bit.'

By the time 'Karma Chameleon' went to number one on the
US *Billboard* chart on 25 January 1984 – their first proper American number one, although 'Do You Really Want To Hurt Me'
had hit the top slot in the rival *Cashbox* chart – it seemed like
George was doing just that. Increasing numbers of fans were
turning up at Culture Club shows dressed, like their British
counterparts, as Boy George clones. It was now even possible to
buy a Hasidic-hatted and dreadlocked Boy George doll. The
pattern was repeated by other groups. When Duran Duran played
Madison Square Gardens in March 1984, you couldn't help
noticing the hundreds of fans sporting John Taylor trilbies. In
fact, the crowd looked and behaved exactly like a British Duran
audience: they waved banners, did their best to outwit the
bouncers and, of course, screamed their lungs out.

With sales of pre-recorded music estimated, in 1983, to have
a retail value of over $2500 million, America accounts for nearly
a *third* of the total world market. In 1983, British music and
British artists occupied a solid and presumably lucrative 35 per
cent of the *Billboard* top 100 in both singles and albums. For
their contribution the individual members of Culture Club are
now all multi-millionaires. So are the members of the two other
top British groups in the USA in 1983: Duran Duran and the
Police.

But George, the boy whose earliest memory is of a longing –
literally – to be a household name, took it all one step further yet.
He didn't stop at becoming a pop star; he became a personality.
'Do You Really Want To Hurt Me' had launched Culture Club
into the charts. Now George set about launching himself into
America's living rooms. In a country like Britain, with a national
media, one *Top of the Pops* appearance had done the trick. In
America, it was harder. As their first American tour snaked its
way round a route of relatively small venues in spring 1983,
George and his American press agents contrived a total media
blitz. America, having initially fallen for his voice, raised its

eyebrows at George's appearance and demanded explanations. George provided them – to the tune of about twenty or thirty interviews a day for papers, magazines, TV and radio stations. On 23 January 1984, he and Annie Lennox appeared side by side on the cover of *Newsweek* (in a photograph originally shot for *Smash Hits*). A few weeks later he was interviewed by Joan Rivers on the *Tonight* show. By then Culture Club weren't just selling records to screaming pop crazy teenagers; they were selling them to everyone. George, as *Rolling Stone* put it, had won the Liberace vote.

America has a culture of fame underpinned by an all-pervasive mythology of success, a nation where John Hinckley Jnr can shoot a former B-movie actor turned president and describe his action as 'a movie starring me'. The famous become brand names; the heroes of free enterprise. George had taken the Americans on at the game they play best and acquitted himself admirably. He was now a star in the grand tradition – regardless of record sales, a bigger star than just about anyone else in pop music save Michael Jackson. In 1983 George became the kind of media-made celebrity who, in Daniel Boorstin's words, is 'famous for being well-known'. His notoriety will persist long after Culture Club are forgotten.

Indeed, even now, people often tend to forget that the other three members of the group exist. In early 1984, Culture Club were voted Best Newcomers in the American Grammy awards. When they turned up at the London TV studio from which they were to telecast an appearance accepting the award from Joan Rivers, Jon looked around, saw only two stools set up in front of the cameras and realized that they were expecting George alone to receive it. He was furious. George took up the case and refused to go on unless the band appeared too. In the end, they stood behind him as he perched on his stool. By now in a belligerent mood, George accepted the award with the words: 'Thank you, America. You have taste, style and you know a good drag queen when you see one.' The American media haven't stopped calling him a 'self-acclaimed drag queen' since and for the first time a crack appeared in the homely, lovable façade that George usually projects.

It was his first big mistake with the media.

The pop explosion of the 1960s was linked to deep social changes that were then taking place: changes in class structure, sexual behaviour and political beliefs. It had to do with more than just the way people walked, talked, dressed and danced, though all that was part of it too. In the 1960s, the young British working class was suddenly upwardly mobile. They had cash and they spent it, allowing the phenomenal growth of the youth market. And the easy-going affluence of the period was certainly linked to the liberalization of sexual attitudes. Casual sex simply went hand in hand with spontaneous consumption. On both sides of the Atlantic there was something of a sense of chaos, of the increasing redundancy of traditional values. In Britain, the Profumo scandal and the end of thirteen years of Tory rule, and in America, the civil rights campaigns and the Kennedy assassination, all fanned the fire of the new movement.

When the Beatles appeared, Britain was in the throes of a radical transformation. No longer top nation, it was grudgingly getting used to its new, muted role in America's shadow. But though Britannia had ceased to rule the waves, she could at least have a stab at ruling the airwaves. The empire struck back with pop music – selling rhythm and blues back to the land which spawned it – and the Beatles' very success was at least as exciting as their music. In Britain – and later in America also – the mood of the new beat music was part and parcel of the mood of the nation. It was an era in which Britain dreamed of eternal youth and endless material abundance and the Beatles conquering America seemed just about to sum it all up.

And the pop explosion of the 1980s? The redundancy of traditional values – even given the moral backlash on both sides of the Atlantic – matters less in Thatcher's Britain than the redundancy of a large part of the workforce. These days, social mobility – especially, but by no means exclusively, among the young – is more likely to mean a downward spiral into a new, helpless poverty than a steady progress up and out. On one level, the supremacy of fizzy pop simply reflects the fact that younger teenagers, still supported by their parents and without independent money problems, are better able to afford records than their low-paid or jobless elder brothers and sisters.

If Britain in the 1960s was in a dream, then Britain in the

1980s is locked in a nightmare from which, we are assured by Thatcher, there will be no awakening. No longer top nation? Britain is probably no longer even in the top ten. If the chirpy, irreverent style of the early Beatles reflected the then-growing confidence of youth, then the androgynous style and twisting of gender that characterized the groups which made it in America this time round evidences contemporary confusion. Not just about sex roles, but about roles of all kinds. About Britain's role in the world, even. Who can be surprised that in the depths of a depression, pop takes an escapist turn? And anyway, those who attack the New Pop for its superficiality and lack of lyrical punch tend to forget that some of the greatest pop songs of all time, those that won over America far more spectacularly than 'Karma Chameleon' or 'Hungry Like The Wolf', were, as writer Lester Bang put it, 'all "yeah, yeah, yeah!" and that was what made the moment precious'.

British pop music is no longer an optimistic, joyful reaching-out. It's become more of a carefully calculated digging-in. Certainly, pop music is still a prime means for working-class kids to move up, out and make some cash – but these days it's also a reputable career for the sons and daughters of the middle classes too. In 1982, Jim Kerr of Simple Minds talked to me about the conversations he and other bands from out of London would have in the bar of the Columbia Hotel in Lancaster Gate – the place where every second division pop group on the way up seems to stay.

'There's a new realism now in the pop world. I hope it gets even more realistic as it goes on. I don't mean everybody wants to be like the man in the street – it's always good to have oddballs around – but if you sit in our hotel and listen to bands talking, it's like being in a band is a respectable profession these days. When kids go up to their parents and say "I want to be in a band", their parents should say, "Why, son, that's great".'

New realism? In the late 1960s, the Beatles formed their Apple group of companies on a wave of idealism. With hindsight it looks to have been a sophisticated organization for the essentially simple purpose of giving money away. You try and catch a British pop group doing anything like that these days. Critics have often dismissed the New Pop as 'Thatcherite' or 'Falklands Pop'. In some ways that's a profoundly stupid description. Culture Club aside, the consensus among today's pop musicians is broadly left of centre. Even Andy Taylor of Duran Duran – the group most usually lumbered with the 'Thatcherite' tag – was recently heard remarking that it made him 'sick to watch what she's doing to the country'. But in some ways, the tag makes sense. 'Falklands Pop' is at least vaguely appropriate for a phenomenon that's been conquering 'territories' (as the record companies call foreign markets) all over the world, even if the spectacle of George and others camping it up a storm on television was a refreshingly long way from that of 'Our Boys' battling away in the South Atlantic. Thatcher's whole style is essentially masculine. That of Boy George is, of course, no such thing.

But the entrepreneurial style of today's pop artists-as-businessmen – and Jon Moss, for example, is an entrepreneur in the classic free enterprise mould; someone whose talent is in organizing the talent around him to make something happen – seems perfectly to fit the Thatcherite ideal of how to revitalize the economy. Remember that after the 1983 Grammy awards, the House of Commons put an approving motion before Parliament:

This House congratulates Culture Club, the Police, Duran Duran and other British stars on their success in the Grammy awards; and acknowledge the enormous pleasure they bring to millions of people around the world and the exports they and their industry achieve for the United Kingdom.

Such opinions are not, however, simply the province of the Right. In the 1960s, Labour Prime Minister Harold Wilson – always astute when it came to PR – awarded the Beatles MBEs in recognition of their services to British industry. And at the BPI awards on 9 February 1985, Labour leader Neil Kinnock, who, apeing the activities of his pop-conscious predecessor, had appeared in a Tracey Ullman video and on a platform with Billy Bragg, was along to present an award.

'I think it's very important,' he replied to an invitation to comment on the record industry in the light of both its earnings abroad and its activities in the UK. 'It may indeed be the last British industry with vitality. I hope it isn't.'

M U S I C

Through green Bavarian fields and a grey mid-morning drizzle, the Culture Club coach cruises towards the German-Austrian border at Braunau, Hitler's birthplace. It is 16 September 1983. The group have just returned from an American tour, 'Karma Chameleon' has just leapt straight into the British top ten and *Colour By Numbers* is just about to be released. This afternoon, they will be recording an appearance for the German pop show, *Bananas*. It's just another promotional trip and everyone is dog-tired. Jon stares out at the countryside, cracking the odd nervous joke about Nazis and wondering what it would be like to be a farmer. George, in high spirits, chatters and jokes and directs the occasional bitchily-barbed remark at Roy, who tries to laugh it off and says little. Mikey, curled up at the back, still hasn't woken up yet.

I'd heard a little of *Colour By Numbers* in a cab on the way to Heathrow the day before. At 'Mister Man', the midddle-aged black driver had pricked up his ears. 'Is *that* Boy George's voice?' he asked approvingly. But now, on the coach, with George sat next to me and chattering away about each song, I'm hearing it in its entirety for the first time.

'Listen,' George touches my elbow when the opening Motown beat of 'Church Of The Poison Mind' belts out. He grins, waits for the cue and then sings Stevie Wonder over the top: 'Uptight, everything is already, outta sight . . .' It fits perfectly.

Jon, sticking his head over the top of a nearby seat, raises an eyebrow. 'I'd keep quiet about that if I were you.'

But George has no intention of doing any such thing. He points out a bit of the melody of 'It's A Miracle' that comes from Gilbert O'Sullivan. When the flute comes in at the beginning of 'Stormkeeper', he smiles and says: 'That sounds like Men At Work'. George isn't ashamed of this borrowing. Far from it. He seems positively proud. As we listen on, the names of those to whom Culture Club have accorded the sincerest form of flattery continue to tumble out.

In September 1983, Culture Club were just scaling the final slopes on the way to the peak of their popularity. *Colour By Numbers* went on to establish itself as one of the classic pop albums, not just of the 1980s, but of all time. So familiar has it now become, I can no longer spot most of the references George pointed out. Their steals were pretty skilful and Culture Club made them their own. But as George talked that day, I wrote all the names down in my notebook:

Paul Simon, Blue Mink, Steely Dan, Carole King, Gilbert O'Sullivan, Michael Jackson, Martha Reeves and the Vandellas, Stevie Wonder, Daryl Hall and John Oates, Shalamar, The Isleys, Men At Work, Johnny Nash, 'MacArthur Park', Crosby, Stills, Nash and Young . . .

Ah, the fine art of plunder and pastiche. You know, mix 'n' match. 'We just want to write good songs,' is how Culture Club, and indeed just about every other New Pop group, describe their musical intent. And without 'good songs' it's unlikely that Culture Club, charismatic and controversial lead singer or no, would have got very far at all. On the other hand, the same could be said of just about any successful white British pop group since the Beatles – exemplars of all this 'good', i.e. commercial, songwriting. What counts is where the bits and bobs that go into the crafting of those songs come from, why they're mixed and how they're matched.

The situation currently is a complex tangle of musical cross-fertilization. Pop music is now, in all its forms, more based on self-conscious recycling and referencing than at any other point in its brief but chequered history. At times it seems like simply everything exists between ironic quotation marks. It's getting out of hand.

At one extreme you still have the classical phenomenon of a group or artist (usually White) modelling whole phases of their careers on the work of some illustrious predecessor (usually Black). In the past there was, say, Janis Joplin trying to be Bessie Smith or Willie Mae Thornton. Now we have Kevin Rowland of Dexys Midnight Runners as Otis Redding, Alison Moyet as Billie Holiday, Gary Numan as David Bowie or Prince as Little Richard. within Duran Duran you have Simon le Bon wanting to be Jim Morrison and Andy Taylor wanting to be Jeff Beck, while Frankie Goes To Hollywood's Brian Nash wants to be Andy Taylor.

At the other extreme, the technology of electronic instruments has developed to such an extent that it is possible to 'sample' a sound, any sound, and then play it on a keyboard. A Fairlight CMI or an Emulator can be used to make music out of *anything* – the noise of breaking glass, cars starting, whatever – but most typically are used to nick a noise off one record and put it on another. Having mastered the operation of one of these instruments, it's child's play to have, say, Duane Eddy's guitar and James Brown's voice on the same record. Stacks of records have been made using the drum sound from David Bowie's 'Let's Dance'. Producer Trevor Horn, a master of this game and once a member of the Art Of Noise ensemble who make whole records out of sampled sounds, is reputedly fond of using the drum sound of the late John Bonham from Led Zeppelin. Just about every producer in the Western world has used the orchestral 'whoomph' effect first toyed with, I believe, by hip-hop producer Arthur Baker. It's possible, in other words, to mix and match at an almost microscopic level.

Somewhere in between these two poles, you have a group like

Culture Club. Simply listening to their first three hit singles – as the light lover's reggae of 'Do You Really Want To Hurt Me' was followed by the neo-Philadelphia balladry of 'Time' and then the big Motown beat of 'Church Of The Poison Mind' – was like flipping backwards through the pages of some glossy coffee-table book on the history of black music. A glance down the British charts any week in the early 1980s – disregarding all the medleys and cover versions and scratch records that offer still another angle on all this – reveals white pop based in or borrowing from, well, you name it: soul (in all its forms), jazz (ditto), African (likewise), British, Irish and American folk, Latin, Euro–disco, rhythm and blues, rock and roll, avant-garde classical, reggae, ska, hip-hop, Chinese, Japanese, Indian and God knows what else, including, of course, an indigenous pop tradition that was in any case based initially on a variety of black musics.

Confused? You damn well ought to be. Except the pop process has this uncanny knack of embracing anything and everything and making it all sound perfectly natural. Still, reference-spotting has become a favourite game among both music critics and the discerning public. 'That's "Taxman"', by the Beatles!' everyone cried when the Jam's 'Start!' first came out. 'Good God, it's Peter Gabriel's "Solsbury Hill"!' was the initial reaction to Howard Jones' 'New Song'. 'Hey, that's, "Re-united", by Peaches and Herb!' came the chorus when Wham!'s 'Last Christmas' first landed on the *Smash Hits* turntable. Lawsuits proliferate. Kraftwerk's publishers got $20,000 out of Tommy Boy records when Arthur Baker used their 'Trans-Europe Express' riff on Afrika Bambaataa's 'Planet Rock'. Ray Parker Jnr's theme from 'Ghostbusters' inspired not one, but two lawsuits: one claiming it was nicked from M's 'Pop Muzik', another that it was filched from 'I want A New Drug' by Huey Lewis and the News. There have been scores of such cases, even one involving Culture Club's 'Karma Chameleon'.

'Plagiarism,' says George, 'is one of my favourite words. Culture Club is the most sincere form of plagiarism in modern music – we just do it better than most.'

Plagiarism is in fact the favourite word of most of the New Pop groups. It's just that most of them don't like to admit it.

When the New Pop first began crawling from the wreckage of punk in the late 1970s and early 1980s, it looked like electronic music was going to be its mainstay. Among the new groups was a preponderance of synthesizer-based outfits: Orchestral Manoeuvres in the Dark, Depeche Mode, Soft Cell, the Human League, Heaven 17, Ultravox and Visage. Even Duran Duran and Spandau Ballet at first seemed to be electronic pop groups. Futurists, they were labelled, with Gary Numan – at least in terms of chart success – their founding father.

The synthesizer had actually been around in usable form since Robert Moog designed his first transistorized machine in 1964. For the next few years, however, people only used it as an extension of the conventional keyboard. In Britain in 1972, Roxy Music were the first to demonstrate a different tack. Brian Eno matched Bryan Ferry's camp, reference-ridden mix of glitter and 1950s Americana with a lot of startlingly abstract synthesized bleeps and whistles. Roxy's influence, as pioneers of imaginative electronics, self-conscious referencing and ironic musical quotation marks, remains huge. Duran Duran, Japan and the Human League are among the many in their debt.

In Germany, a country with no rock 'n' roll tradition of its own, there were loads of groups experimenting with the new technology. The most influential was Kraftwerk, whose 1974 'Autobahn' was a huge disco hit. Synthesizers, it seemed, were well suited to disco. Stevie Wonder began fiddling with them in 1972. George McRae's 'Rock You Baby', a huge international hit and one of the first disco records, popularized the drum machine in 1974. In Munich in 1976, Giorgio Moroder and Pete Bellotte began collaborating with Donna Summer on pioneering electronic disco records like 'Love To Love You Baby' and 'I Feel Love'. Around this time, David Bowie and Brian Eno began working together in Berlin on a trilogy of largely electronic albums. Well, if it was good enough for Bowie . . .

All-synthesizer groups began proliferating in Britain as punk faded into the do-it-yourself independent scene. The synthesizer was, in fact, the ultimate do-it-yourself accessory. Who needed to spend years learning an instrument when you could programme a machine to do it for you? As people experimented with the technology, an electronic underground, comprising groups like

Cabaret Voltaire and Throbbing Gristle, began to emerge and a grey, gloomy style was established. The first to break into the charts with electronic pop was Gary Numan. Sheffield's Human League probably began to kick themselves. They'd been experimenting with electronic pop for ages but had yet to find the right commercial formula.

By this time, singer Philip Oakey had learnt an important lesson. 'In the end I'm not sure that synthesizers themselves are that important,' he commented in 1982. 'They are just tools. If you're trying for pop success, the important thing is the song.'

In that sense – and Oakey, who always talked about writing 'proper' songs, 'like Abba or Earth, Wind and Fire', is right – the idea of electronic pop is a bit of a red herring. Depeche Mode, Soft Cell and others all found fame and fortune by playing classically-structured pop songs with new-fangled instruments. But the technology was important. By obviating technique, it allowed a lot of non-musicians to enter the fray. By providing new noises, it gave early New Pop a sound quite different from what had gone before. As old-style synthesizers give way to the even newer sound-sampling instruments, new technology continues to be integral to the New Pop. Even Culture Club, one of the least electronic groups in the arena, have used Fairlight sounds on their records.

Long after the New Pop had been picked up by the kids in America, the US critical establishment was still dismissing it off-handedly as 'disco made pretty'. A silly line of argument, this, harking as it does back to the late 1970s period of 'Disco Sucks' T-shirts when it was still largely held by white American rock fans that Black music was incapable of any sophistication of expression. That, one supposes, goes double for a dressed-up white limey version of a Black American form, even though the 'good song' structure of most New Pop records has bugger all to do with the linear form of the classic disco cut. The main thing that's been borrowed is the beat.

A curious irony here, anyhow. White British working-class kids – in clubland and elsewhere – have always treasured Black music – jazz, soul, funk and reggae – with a keep-the-faith fervour entirely lacking on the other side of the Atlantic, even though that's where most of this music comes from. White British pop music and subculture has always kept up such a dialogue with Black music and style that Dick Hebdige, in his book *Subculture*, describes their interplay as a 'phantom history of race relations since the War'.

The dialogue – which until recently was almost entirely one way – has actually been going on even longer than that. On both sides of the Atlantiç, jazz was feeding into the mainstream of popular culture from the 1920s and 1930s. Britain, too, had its swing big bands playing a White, laundered version of jazz: Ted Heath, Joe Loss, Ambrose and their respective orchestras all grew up while the Musicians Union was still banning Americans from playing in Britain. In the 1950s there was a sort of British beatnik, grooving not to be-bop, but to Miles Davis, Coltrane and 'cool jazz'. Ronnie Scott was the British version and the music was known as modern, as opposed to trad. More of a suburban form, trad was a watered-down recreation of New Orleans jazz. Louis Armstrong was the model, Chris Barber and Acker Bilk the local heroes.

Later in the 1950s came the teds, bringing with them their fascination with Black rhythm and blues and its White American equivalent. That, of course, fed into the whole British beat explosion of the early 1960s and the first bout of American astonishment at having their music dusted off, vibed up and flogged back to them. From here on in, the stakes were raised. The Brits didn't just have to buy and copy American culture. Sharing a language, they were capable of taking it apart, tinkering with it and actually improving on it. The Beatles and the Stones seemed to have proved that.

Elsewhere in the early 1960s, the mods were discovering soul and founding a dance underground that would continue on in a broken line until it got mixed up with the early days of punk. Mod fragmented into the fashion-conscious crowd who merged with early hippy on the one hand, and on the other into the hard end who by the late 1960s had evolved into skinheads. The skins took a large part of their style and practically all of their music from West Indian immigrants. They stomped to ska and then reggae, until it became too drenched in marijuana and mysticism to make much sense to them.

By the late 1960s and early 1970s, a substantial rift had developed between White and Black musics. In the wake of the psychedelic experiments, rock fans began touting their music as Art. It 'progressed'. Its lofty pretensions were 'meaningful'. It moved deeper into the studio and further away from the dancefloor. Black music, from which white rock had been born, was held to be inadequate for the now essential task of *artistic expression*. This was largely a class thing, for while the grammar school boys toted their Yes and Genesis LPs, their working-class counterparts still tended to seek solace with their Black neighbours down the disco. White music only began to move back towards black in the latter days of glam rock as Bryan Ferry acknowledged his debt to Motown and Stax and Bowie began playing 'plastic soul' on 'Young Americans'.

Then along came punk and, in its courtship with reggae, something completely different happened. Reggae was an extreme music. More like be-bop than Motown, it was pronounced and proscriptive in its Blackness, designed to be almost completely incomprehensible to the average white listener. Punk didn't try and imitate it. Instead, it established itself in a kind of complementary opposition. Where reggae was languorous and rooted in bass, punk was manic and trebly. Where reggae communicated with metaphor and allusion, punk applied sarcasm and raw polemic. Contrary to appearances, the music wasn't really opposed. Punk just wanted a riot of its own and was happy to come together with reggae in the Rock Against Racism concerts of the late 1970s. Punk, argued Dick Hebdige, was an *ethnic* white music. As such, it profoundly affected the relationship between White pop and Black music.

A lot of soul boys had been swept up into punk. As it fragmented, they dived back into the discos. The time of all the post-punk independent experiments – from 1978 to 1980 – was also the heyday of disco music: Chic and Funkadelic, and Michael Jackson's and Kool and the Gang. It was inevitable that this would begin feeding back into the white pop mainstream and, sure enough, soon it did. Here were the beginnings of the New Pop. Duran Duran formed on the premise of combining the simplicity and solidity of the Chic rhythm section with the raw energy of the Sex Pistols. Spandau Ballet, once they'd got over their initial stab at Euro-disco, settled back into their soul boy roots and began attempting a British funk with 'Chant No. 1'. Throughout 1981 all sorts of white 'funk' groups appeared, most of them in retrospect the sheerest travesty of the term. Although the New Pop, as it developed, took on board a world of influences, that long-cherished Black American dance music remains its principal source.

For the most part that means Motown and related Black pop. Motown's hummable melodies, 'good song' structure and punchy beat makes it perfect material for the New Pop. Wham! seem to be basing their entire career on it. Other, less clearly commercial, kinds of 1960s Black music are being mined by groups like The Style Council, Kane Gang and Dexys Midnight Runners. None of that lot, however, seem capable of doing so without inflating the practice with a spurious aura of abstract 'commitment' supposedly lacking in groups with a more frivolous approach to what they mix and match. By and large the New Pop plunders more eclectically: a Motown melody here, a disco rhythm there and a few hip-hop effects, say, to top it all off.

But something else is going on. For the first time, Black music seems to be taking as much from White pop as White pop is taking from Black. In Britain, Black groups have begun to style and market themselves much in the manner of White bands. This may in part be a response to simple market pressures, but it began at the time all the White funk groups appeared. In New York in 1982 and 1983, hip-hop went into a phase of borrowing from European electronic music. This move, initially based around the artists and producers of Tommy Boy records, was picked up by everyone. It seemed to provide the spur that moved the music out of Manhattan and into the global mainstream. By 1985, hip-hop groups like Run DMC and the Def Jam stable were plundering furiously from heavy White rock. In more mainstream Black music, this has been gathering pace for a while. Giorgio Moroder's late 1970s work with Donna Summer – *Hot Stuff* and all that – was often rock-based. A lot of producers have since picked up on that style. Michael Jackson, having made a record with Paul McCartney, went on to do a rock track in 'Beat It' complete with a furious Eddie Van Halen guitar solo. Prince does this kind of thing all the time. While White pop has been sounding ever lighter and more Black, Black music has been getting heavier and ever more like White rock. It's a pleasing irony. This may only in part have to do with the way punk established itself as the first authentically White ethnic music and therefore, in the larger scheme of things, made it all plunderable, but John Lydon making the heavy, rock-based 'World Destruction' with hip-hop king Afrika Bambaataa was a telling collaboration. On the other hand, Culture Club getting the idea for the guitar solo on 'Miss Me Blind' from Michael Jackson's 'Beat It' was nothing short of hilarious.

The miscegenation between White and Black, Britain and America is now so complex it's damn near impossible to unravel. It'll get worse. Only one thing is certain: crossover logic underlies it all. In a shrinking and increasingly fragmented world record market, the surest way to make big bucks is to scoop up as many different markets as possible. 'Beat It' was designed to capture the rock crowd as well as the disco set. So was 'Miss Me Blind'. Both scoop up the pop market in the middle. Chaka Khan's 'I Feel For You', dismissed by the singer herself as 'the pits', aimed to unite pop, soul, disco and hip-hop and, judging by the way it zipped up charts all over the globe, seems to have done the job admirably.

As the nascent markets of Asia, Africa and Latin America are increasingly brought into the industry's long-term plans, this kind of thing can only increase. As events like the massive, three-day rock festival in Rio in January 1985 and Wham!'s pioneering trip to China in April become more and more commonplace, as all the new technology in music and communications stirs the global melting-pot faster and faster – making world media events like Live-Aid possible – there are no longer any absolute boundaries between musics, races and styles.

Corny it may sound, but the whole world is becoming a culture club.

Early in 1984, my brother's jeep broke down in northern Tanzania. He was hundreds of miles from the nearest city, right in the middle of Masai territory. The Masai are at best indifferent to Whites and at worst outrightly hostile. Martin was understandably nervous about approaching the locals, but plucked up the courage to seek help in an isolated settlement. Shuffling into the village store, he heard a familiar tune booming from an imported Japanese ghetto blaster and couldn't help but laugh. All the locals present burst out laughing too, which broke the ice and allowed him to get the help he needed.

In the shadow of Mount Kilimanjaro, the tune playing was 'Karma Chameleon'.

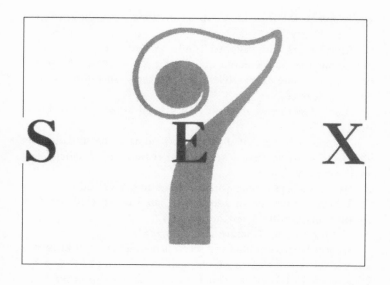

SEX

'Excuse me, love,' quips George blithely at a dark-suited Japanese salaryman as he pushes past into the dining car. The salaryman, uncomprehending, bows slightly. A crowd of waitresses stand and stare. 'I'd like some soup,' George decides as he, I and official Culture Club photographer André Csillag sit down at a table. ''Ere, *Blanche!*' he calls coquettishly to the nearest waitress. 'I'd like some soup.' At once, the waitresses all clap their hands over their mouths and dissolve into helpless giggles. André and I, bemused by the context of George's camperie, start giggling too.

After a lot more gesticulating, giggling and Blancheing, George finally gets his bowl of soup. And then, as he cups it in his hands and takes a first sip, he starts giggling as well. 'I want to ask you a really cheeky question,' he peeks at me over the soup bowl, bright-eyed and mischievous. 'But I don't really know if I should . . .'

'Go on,' I shrug, knowing full well what's coming. 'Ask away.'

'Well,' George giggles a little more. 'I don't know why because

91

you're not in the least bit camp or anything but, you know, em . . . are you gay?'

André roars with laughter. Only yesterday I'd been telling him about the time George quizzed me similarly on the sexual orientation of one of my colleagues. My reply, therefore, is more or less rehearsed.

'Look, George, what would you say if I asked *you* that question?'

The point being that if *he*'s always going to be so damn coy about his sexuality then I see no real reason why *I* should give anything away.

'Well,' George replies without hesitation. 'Yes and no.'

Which is more of an admission than I'd expected. By now André is practically under the table.

'All right then,' I hazard. 'No and yes.'

George laughs out loud and screams triumphantly. 'I knew it! I knew it!' He's well pleased with himself now. 'I don't know how but I just knew it, I knew it. Blanche! Can I have a cup of tea?'

André, like the waitresses, just carries on giggling.

P op music and sexuality have been so long and so intimately entwined that it seems almost fatuous to mention it. From Elvis Presley's hip movements being censored on the Ed Sullivan Show to Frankie Goes To Hollywood's 'Relax' being banned on British national radio is a gap of twenty-eight years but also, in a way, no distance at all. In the intervening 'permissive' decades, the frontiers of acceptability have been rolled back a little. With the commoditization of sex as part of the leisure industry, the forms and definitions of sexuality available for consumption have broadened, diverged and multiplied. But sexuality's pride of place at the very core of pop has never been challenged, its currency as outrage never devalued. All that's happened is that the exercise has grown a lot more calculating and efficient. Sex might be able to get on without pop music, but pop music certainly still can't get on without sex.

In the New Pop, sex seems, if anything, more important than

ever. In the first place, there is the New Pop's function as the 1980s version of classic teen scream fantasy fodder, the male pop star as sex object and all that. It is probably now more difficult than ever to find fame and fortune in the pop world if you're just not a pretty face. That, of course, is the basis of the commonest 'pretty-pretty pap pop' type criticism of all this, usually hauled out by fans of boys' rock and bloody silly considering that it just reflects the needs of the teenage girls who are the principal buyers of all the records. It also, to an extent, puts men further into the same 'for appearance's sake' position that women have always been in. Which, if not an advance, is at least an interesting step sideways. By the same token, women like Helen Terry and Alison Moyet have proved that you don't necessarily have to be a dolly-bird to have a hit.

In the second place, there is the New Pop's debt to disco. Dance has always been basic to the function and meaning of pop. The dancefloor has always been the most obvious public space for sexual expression through music. Disco, as it evolved throughout the 1970s, emerging from Black clubs before being crucially modified in gay ones, represented the climax of the union between music, dance and eroticism. There was literally nothing else to it. Disco's open-ended rhythms and repetitions, dramatic dives and soaring peaks, consumed at starkly dominating volume and beefed up, perhaps, with a pulsing light show and a whiff of amyl nitrate, aimed to sweep you and your whole body away on a tide of transitory sensation. What lyrics there were bolstered this up with a swathe of associations initially imported from gay culture but applicable to anyone in the sexually mobile 1970s. They were all about looking and feeling good, fleeting romantic contact and unfettered, almost offhand lust. Disco was about sex as something to be consumed. Along with the beat, a lot of this has filtered through into the New Pop. As long as the music is being consumed on a bright, Saturday night dancefloor, it doesn't necessarily matter what the artists *think* they're writing songs about. The audience will make their own meanings.

And in the third place, there is the whole issue of androgyny, the mass proliferation of men in frocks making pop records, 'gender benders' and so forth. In the beginning, there was George. After him, the deluge: Marilyn, Pete Burns of Liverpool's Dead Or Alive, Dee Snider of the USA's Twisted Sister. Briefly, there was also a chap called Tasty Tim who made one record before everyone forgot about him again. And then of course there was the fabulous Divine, former underground film actor turned disco star. His one, butt-slapping appearance on *Top Of The Pops* doing 'You Think You're A Man' effectively put an end to his British television career and, in a way, stemmed the gender-bending tide. What could follow that?

But at the phenomenon's height, in 1983, it seemed to be going on all over the place. Annie Lennox in a man's suit. Dustin Hoffman in *Tootsie*. Even Margaret Thatcher as more of a man than the rest of the Tory Cabinet put together. Androgyny spilled all over the daily papers, who coined that ugly term 'gender bender' and went to town, reporting any detail they could find or make up about George and Marilyn's endless bickering. It brimmed over into high street fashion, with suits for women and skirts and diamante for men. In a curious kind of double bend, all this concentration on the gender of clothing worked the other way too, with a lot of men picking up on an exaggeratedly masculine style of dress that actually came from the clone look of the gay scene.

And, of course, none of this was new at all, anyway. George knew this:

'All I've got to say is Elton John did it years before I did.'

So did Marilyn:

'I was quite shocked really that [the press] could be so stupid. You just expect that, after Danny La Rue and Quentin Crisp and God knows who else, someone would be able to accept someone with a bit of old make-up. England's like such a bunch of old drag queens anyway. If you pick up a history book . . . I'm quite tame compared to a lot of people.'

Flipping back through that history book, we find Marc Almond mincing about all over the place a good year before George appeared in view. Then there were all the new romantics, so sexually confused or confusing they were almost neuter. A few pages before that, we find punk in all its fish-net, fetishistic glory. Then there's the chapter titled 'Glam': Bowie, Marc Bolan, Alice Cooper, the New York Dolls and the curious phenomenon of all the brickies in drag, like Sweet, Slade and the Glitter Band. In the same period, Elton John and Queen appeared. There was also shown on British television about that time a documentary

94

play about the life of one Quentin Crisp. 'Blind with mascara and dumb with lipstick', Crisp had been parading the streets of London since the 1920s and was now 'one of the stately homos of England'. In his 1968 autobiography, *The Naked Civil Servant*, he noted that 'by an unlucky chance, the symbols which I had adopted forty years earlier to express my sexual type had become the uniform of all young people'. At the time, hippy men with long hair were causing a lot of 'is it a boy or a girl?' type outrage. Back a little further and we find the Rolling Stones camping it up a storm and being roundly condemned for effeminacy. They even, on the American sleeve and in the promo film for 'Have You Seen Your Mother, Baby, Standing In The Shadow?', appeared in full drag.

Flip back further still and we find a whole chapter on Little Richard, the original Queen of Rock and Roll. One of his best known songs, 'Lucille', was written about a female impersonator in his home town of Macon, Georgia. He introduced make-up to pop music. He influenced everyone from the Beatles and Stones to Elton John, who remarked: 'When I saw Little Richard standing on the piano, all lights, sequins and energy, I decided then and there that I was going to be a rock and roll piano player.'

When Little Richard's records began to sell, there was worry about how his wildly sexual show would go down with White middle America.

'We were breaking through the racial barrier,' he remembers in Charles White's excellent memoir. 'The white kids had to hide my records cos they daren't let their parents know they had them in the house. We decided my image should be crazy and way-out so that the adults would think I was harmless. I'd appear in one show dressed as the Queen of England and in the next as the Pope.'

Before Little Richard there was Liberace. And before Liberace, the history of drag, transvestism and dressing up stretches back for centuries. George is fond of bracketing himself in the grand tradition of British eccentricity, citing the make-up and powdered wigs of the Restoration as an obvious antecedent. There is, in short, nothing new under the sun.

95

In a sense, what George did with his 'look' was the same as Little Richard had attempted while dressing as the Pope. He wanted to appear harmless. He wanted his clothes to cloak his homosexuality. At the time of Culture Club's Heaven concert in mid-1982, he hadn't quite cracked it yet. Looking angular and skinny, with a pair of industrial shades clapped round his eyes and a sulky, almost resentful look on his face, he seemed stern and strangely sinister. By the time of 'Do You Really Want To Hurt Me', he'd changed subtly, but completely. The shades were gone, he'd put on a bit of weight, he smiled all the time and suddenly he'd become the cuddly, lovable Boy George who had the public and the media eating out of the palm of his hand.

George has always employed an ingeniously stealthy approach to his presentation of self. Apparently poised precariously between boy and girl, between hetero, gay or bisexual, his strategy has been the simple one of keeping everyone guessing. Close questioning usually elicits affronted dismissal ('Does it matter?'), bare-faced lies ('I haven't slept with anyone for the last two years.') or artful dodging.

Is he bisexual?

'No, I never have to buy sex.'

When was the last time he slept with someone?

'I never sleep when I have sex. I usually try to stay awake.'

George, in fact, does his best to come across as almost sexless. He'd rather go to bed with a teddy bear than an Action Man. He prefers a cup of tea to sex – although, when doing the voice-over for his Madame Tussaud's dummy, he appended that last one-liner with a quick 'and if you believe that you'll believe anything'.

Still, whatever the papers say, George has managed to stifle any real outrage at his appearance by constructing an aura of childlike innocence. Even at his most attractive, with his ribbons and bows, he looked less like a sex object than a present waiting to be unwrapped: a nice little doll, with accompanying warm and cosy Christmas feelings. What could be less threatening than that? With George's comments on sex always framed within a very traditional, conservative morality – that sex means nothing without love and, by implication, marriage – there is left no reason in the world why anyone should lock up their sons when Culture Club come to town, still less their daughters.

In all this, and particularly in his refusal to come out, George is worlds away from the mainstream gay scene. Clearly, someone like him has little time and less sympathy for a culture which, if only superficially, still tends to submerge individual identity in a sea of identical moustaches, short haircuts, black leather and denim. The gay community, meanwhile, has returned the compliment. Culture Club are not, for example, well liked in San Francisco. In London, around the time of 'Do You Really Want To Hurt Me', George was given a good ticking-off by a clone at a North London gay disco-pub. The chap reckoned George, by using the word 'poof', was betraying gays when he should be defending them. He'd been beaten up just for wearing a Gay Pride badge. So what, George replied, *he'd* been beaten up for wearing a Mother's Pride badge. George flounced out and minutes later the club was attacked by club-wielding skinheads. The militant gay pop group Bronski Beat also criticized George for not being 'supportive' enough. I put this to George once, along with the information that the father of the Bronski singer Jimmy Somerville hadn't dared tell any of his friends when his son first appeared on television. He was worried Jimmy would be decked out in ribbons and frocks, 'just like Boy George'.

'So in that case my message is far more potent than theirs, isn't it?' George snapped back. 'Let me tell you that what I'm doing is far ahead of what they're doing. I don't try to walk around in a check shirt and I don't try to look normal. I'm not hiding anything. That's the underlying statement. What I'm doing, whether I say anything or not, is making people accept effeminate men. I'm making people accept it into their homes and into their kitchens. I'm not supportive because I don't have to be. I support my own beliefs. And my own beliefs are being sold in large quantities around the world. To normal people. So, his father answered the question, didn't he?

'I've been turned away from more gay clubs than anyone I know, with a statement like: "You're embarrassing to us. Go away." I'm far more open than anybody is about what I am as a person and what I represent.'

What George would say he represents is a freedom from the limits of conventional masculinity.

97

'Like my song "Mr Man". It's in your head. You don't have to be a man. Men weren't born to drink beer. I don't think it's being gay that's the problem. It's being effeminate. It's being not manly that's the problem. You see, when people accept Boy George they're accepting a million things about themselves. They're not accepting that I'm gay or straight; they're accepting that men can act in a different way from how they're expected to act. Those barriers can not be broken down with one word, with "I'm gay". It's a long, long hard fight.'

All of which is very sensible but yet begs a lot of questions. It's difficult to believe that George isn't at least in part motivated by the fact that keeping everyone guessing makes sound commercial sense. Around the beginning of 1985, George began talking about the conflict between 'Boy George' and 'Boy Georgina'. Boy George, he made it clear, was the boy-next-door George the public knew, the persona groomed to international acceptability with the help of Jon Moss and Tony Gordon: interesting but unthreatening. Boy Georgina was the George that George felt himself to be: a much more outrageous character, one who queened around in public with stilletoes and hats and was rude to people precisely when and how he felt like it. It was Boy Georgina who, for example, turned up at the Royal Albert Hall Frank Sinatra concert with a bloke called Tranny Paul crammed inelegantly into a rubber bathing suit on her arm. I had tea with Jon Moss around this time and it was clear that he was worried about George getting 'seedy' or 'threatening'. He felt George couldn't turn around and behave contrary to his carefully cultivated public image without his fans seeing it as some kind of betrayal, and maybe he was right. At the time, during the build-up to the 1984 Culture Club Christmas British tour, there were a lot of arguments going on in the group around this. Jon and Tony Gordon wanted to curb Georgina. George wanted to let her loose.

'There's a constant battle to decide which is the most prominent,' George told Paul Gambaccini on a televized interview, 'and it always ends up being Boy George – *drat*!'

If it's Boy George who belongs to Culture Club and Jon Moss, then it's Georgina who camps about the globe with Marilyn. At times, the pair of them seem like nothing more than a couple of bickering rent boys, their arguments – like any bout of bitchery you might hear in a run-of-the-mill gay bar – broadcast as if through some freak of the media across the world. Georgina is a queen of a particular kind: temperamental, theatrical and half in the closet. Someone who is absolutely obsessed about who's gay and who isn't and who, as often as not, is snooty about those who are. If the conventional gay scene is not to George's liking, then that's at least in part because Georgina doesn't want a 'poof'. She wants a 'real man'.

The 'real man' in George's life is, of course, Jon Moss, someone who, by all accounts, was straight as they come before hooking up with the Boy and who has carried on having the odd heterosexual dalliance ever since. Their relationship has always been crucial to the group. Apart from his skill in whipping Culture Club into a commercial proposition, Jon has actually moulded a hell of a lot of the George we hear in interviews. From him comes much of the intellectual undertow to George's babble. All that stuff about 'strong moral codes', for example. Jon has never got on well with Philip Sallon or Marilyn or any of that crowd, but does seem genuinely to care for George and is keen to keep him on the, um, straight and narrow. If George is now a wilder and less popular character than he used to be, this may in part be because Jon's watchful influence is waning.

In almost every respect, this is a modern echo of a very old phenomenon. In the 1960s, the path to fame and fortune in the world of British pop began with the casting couch. A clique of homosexual managers ruled the roost. Among these were Brian Epstein (Beatles), Robert Stigwood (Bee Gees), Kit Lambert (The Who) and Simon Napier-Bell (Yardbirds, Marc Bolan). Now manager of Wham!, Napier-Bell is the last of them still in the management game. The relationships between these men and their charges were close and vital and kept well under wraps as the teenage horde screamed its knickers down outside. On and off, the phenomenon continued right up to the relationship between Tom Paton and the Bay City Rollers in the mid-1970s and, for all I know, carries on today. Jon's relationship with and influence over George is the New Pop version. It's all within the group. Control over destiny extends even down to this level.

In his hilariously scurrilous memoir of the 1960s music business, *You Don't Have To Say You Love Me*, Simon Napier-Bell had this to say about the Beatles:

'. . . The main secret the Beatles shared was how four tough working-class lads had come to accept the benefit of acting coquettishly for a wealthy middle-class homosexual.

People said their image was that of the boy next door, but it wasn't. To anyone who'd seen it before, their image was instantly identifiable. It was the cool, cocky brashness of a kid who's found himself a sugar-daddy and got set up in Mayfair.

Which puts me, obliquely, in mind of my favourite kind of Culture Club photograph. George will stand, surrounded protectively by these three hunky men dressed up and decked out in the lurex, diamante or leather he's styled for them, pouting and grinning into the camera while they look as butch as possible. His expression says one thing: 'Look what *I've* got, girls!'

F A N S

I t's mid-August 1984, the school holidays are in full swing and outside EMI headquarters at London's Manchester Square, a small group of Duran Duran fans are hanging around hopefully. Today, the grapevine reckons, they might catch a glimpse of Simon le Bon. If there's time, maybe they'll get another autograph, take another picture, the better to fill out their already bulging Duran scrapbooks. And if the great god of all fans is smiling upon them, perhaps they'll even get a quick peck on the cheek. Who knows? They're just passing the time. Waiting to see what happens.

What happens is that Boy George turns up. Blond and bronzed after a holiday in Jamaica, he's with his old friend Philip Sallon, who's just done his first (and last) single for EMI. The Duran fans seethe and hiss. They hate George. He's Duran enemy number one. How dare he slag off *their* group? It is, for these girls, an emotive issue. The self-esteem of individual fans is always tied up with the fortunes of the group they've chosen to follow. By bad-mouthing Duran – particularly his usual line about how they're just selling fantasy, 'all the things that fans *can't* have in life' – George has been belittling them.

Their mood is ugly. They taunt George and set fire to Culture Club pictures and trample them in the gutter. They kick his car and shout that they hate him and call him a 'fat poof'. George, attracted to an argument like a moth to flame, leaps straight into the fray.

'I stand a better chance of sleeping with Simon le Bon than you do, honey!' he snaps at one fan and flounces off.

The fans plot revenge. They decide to pretend George punched one of their number and all take turns lying on the pavement pretending to be unconscious while the others take pictures of them. Janice Cracknell's picture of her friend Alison English turns out looking pretty convincing, so they race down to Fleet Street and sell the story to the *Sun* for the princely sum of £50. It ends up splattered all over the front page of their 15 August edition.

'BOY GEORGE HIT ME SAYS GIRL, 16,' trumpets the headline. 'Pop fans in "fattie" fury.'

The following day, after a lot of justifiably angry denials from George, Alison's parents make her admit she was lying.

Exuberant, inventive, fiercely partisan and often utterly obsessive, the fans are the very foundation of the New Pop. Almost by definition, a New Pop group is one that can lay claim to a fanatical female following. Forget about groups like U2, Simple Minds or Big Country, however successful they might have been both in Britain and abroad over the last few years. They are boys' bands – *rock* bands – and they don't count.

No, the New Pop groups are those like Culture Club, Duran Duran, Wham!, Spandau Ballet, Nik Kershaw, Howard Jones and any others who have fans so devoted they wear their clothes and copy their hair-dos, fans who chase them around in taxis and hound them to their hotels, fans appearing in droves anywhere they know they might show up, fans ferreting out their ex-directory phone numbers and showering them with preposterously lavish presents, fans waving banners and screaming their lungs out at concerts, fans rioting at airports, fans pinching flowers from their parents' front gardens, fans doing extraordinary detective work to locate their addresses and then hanging around outside them, day and night, summer and winter, once they do.

And, of course, fans buying anything and everything even remotely connected with the group. That's the hub of it. That's what makes the millionaires.

Teenage girl fans are both extraordinarily retentive and fiercely competitive. The measure of the true fan's dedication is the number of posters on her wall, the number of scrapbooks she has filled to bursting with pictures and autographs and memorabilia. True fans don't just buy records and concert tickets. They buy videos, posters, watches, badges, T-shirts, scarves, tour programmes, fan club specials, bags, books, magazines, board games, dolls and indeed just about anything that the merchandizing minds can dream up. There is a great mountain of pocket money out there and the New Pop groups are nothing if not sufficient unto the task of shovelling as much of it as possible in the direction of their numbered Swiss bank accounts.

But true fans don't stop at buying and collecting things. When loyal, their loyalty knows no bounds. The devotion of some 'superfans' borders on the pathological. Their rooms are transformed into shrines. Every penny they earn is spent on the object of their obsession, every waking moment spent in contemplation and homage.

Here is Tony Schailer, a Status Quo superfan, talking to *Smash Hits*:

'If I've got a problem, I'll talk to him [Francis Rossi] as if he was in the room with me. It's got to the stage where they're just my life. If I lost my job, it wouldn't bother me. As long as I've got Status Quo, there's something worth carrying on for. I once met Francis at a soundcheck in Brighton. He shook my hand, asked me where I came from and all that lark. My eyes just filled with water. He just said: 'It's OK, mate. Don't worry about it.' It was the best moment of my life so far.'

And that's a boy talking. The devotion of Status Quo fans is probably nothing compared to that of the Duran Duran fans, generally acknowledged – even, grudgingly and jealously, by other pop stars – as the most loyal in the business. Although Duran have never sold as many records as, say, Culture Club, the energy of their fans makes them look much bigger than they are. They vote Duran to the top of the teenage polls, not just in Britain, but all around the world: Australia, the USA, Japan. At *Smash Hits*, if anyone dared to give them a bad review, they would be deluged with vicious hate mail. Duran fans don't just follow the group, they stick up for them. They follow them too, of course. They pop up everywhere. On their 1984 American tour, John Taylor found two under the table in the dressing-room. They'd been there for hours. In his New York hotel room, Andy Taylor found three in his wardrobe. In spring 1983, to record their third album, Duran tried to isolate themselves on the Caribbean island of Montserrat. It didn't work. Some fans even turned up there, having travelled all the way from Britain.

Culture Club have a lot of superfans too. A select group of a dozen or so, christened 'the A-team' by George, follow Culture Club wherever they can, spending literally thousands of pounds of their savings, wages, dole money, whatever, on keeping up with the group. Some of them made it over to America; others have trailed after them around Europe, hitching, sleeping rough, getting drenched, going without food for days just to be near the group. Even with a watchful, caring George to bail them out of trouble when the going gets that little bit too tough, these fans put themselves through hell for Culture Club. And, presumably, they get a lot out of doing so. When George's assistant Bill Button scolded two of the A-team, Margo and Melanie, for once spending about £100 on birthday presents for his boss, Melanie replied: 'We work for our money, we saved for it – so why not? We like spending it on George. We're doing it because *we* get pleasure out of it too.'

But however loyal fans might be, they have also, historically, proved notoriously fickle. What gives a New Pop star sleepless nights? Worrying about the cycle of popularity, that's what.

The cycle of popularity goes something like this: A band is formed, for whatever reason. In the beginning, if they're any good, they have a small, devoted cult following. This is usually based around their home town or within a particular subculture and is enough to bring the group to the attention of the media. Duran Duran, Wham!, Adam Ant, the Human League, Culture Club, Spandau Ballet, Thompson Twins and Howard Jones all started out this way. So, in the past, did David Bowie and Marc Bolan's T. Rex. After a while, if a group is lucky enough, good-looking enough, has a good enough manager and record company, is capable of negotiating the media and can, at the very least, make competent records, they can suddenly burst into mass popularity. At this point, they will no longer be hip, the older music press will begin attacking them and their original fans, feeling abandoned, will wander off home in disgust. Meanwhile, the group milks the market for all it can, very quickly reaching a peak of popularity. And then? Well, it depends. If they tread very carefully, have another large dollop of luck and don't – the commonest mistake – try to cash in too quickly by releasing dozens of similar-sounding records in double-quick succession, then a group might just manage to grow with their audience. This is a delicate and difficult operation. The Beatles and Stones managed it. Gerry and the Pacemakers, say, didn't. Bowie and Roxy Music pulled it off. Marc Bolan fluffed it. Duran Duran look like they might do the trick. Adam Ant cocked it up. In the winter of 1984–5, it looked like Culture Club were cocking it up too.

For those who handle the changeover wrongly, doom lurks in the wings. After all the adulation and success and everything, a group can just . . . disappear. 'Pop', after all, is also the sound of a bubble bursting.

Take the case of Kajagoogoo. In early 1983, missing out the first stage, they were hyped, brilliantly, straight into the charts. Their first single, 'Too Shy', promptly went to number one and in no time at all they looked to be one of pop's biggest attractions with fans who chased them in taxis, hounded them at their hotels, copied their hair-dos, etc. Expeditions set out from *Smash Hits* to go to their concerts, simply to hear the screaming. It was the loudest in living memory. And then, after a few hit singles, a hit album, a sell-out tour and massive success in Europe, the group suddenly sacked their lead singer, Limahl, mainly because the group wanted to be a serious, grown-up act and Limahl was quite content to carry on being a teen-scream sensation. Whatever, it was disastrous. Their fans dropped them without a second thought. Because they'd had a teenage following, no other group of record-buyers would touch them either. Kajagoogoo sank without trace. The only screams left to be heard were those of other pop stars, waking up sweating from hideous nightmares about the same thing happening to them.

Several things are at issue here. One is the faint contempt with which many groups regard the female fans who've made them rich. A lot of pop stars really want to be *rock* stars – like the groups they followed when they were young. The case of Kajagoogoo shows that fans are quite capable of returning the compliment.

Another is the issue of exploitation. 'And as for you poor little cows who buy Duran Duran records,' quoth a John Lydon still living very handsomely off the fact that punk did happen, 'you need serious help 'cause these people are conning you.' A bit rich, perhaps, coming from a chap whose famous last words as a Sex Pistol were: 'Ever had the feeling you've been cheated?' But it also underlines the reason why rock fans and rock critics are so utterly contemptuous of pop music and its screaming fans. They think it's all a con. While they dash about, carefully indulging their freedom of consumer choice on all manner of seminal rock releases – never being conned for a moment, of course – there are all these 'poor little cows' being deluded *en masse* by some monstrous media manipulation that would send a tingle of envy scurrying down Dr Goebbels' long-dead spine. 'Making records for people just because you think that's what they want,' continued Lydon, 'to me that's fascism.'

And to me, that's bollocks.

Implicit in this attitude – and basic to the practice of rock criticism – is the idea that some music is good for you, some music isn't and if all the 'poor little cows' just stopped screaming for a minute and listened to those in the know, then they'd be a lot better off. But pop fans aren't stupid. They know what they want. And ultimately, all the media manipulation in the world isn't going to sell them something they haven't any use for. At the beginning of 1985, with the maximum of ceremony, a new group called the Roaring Boys was launched upon the world. Or at least, there was an attempt. A bunch of good-looking Cambridge graduates, they were backed up by a record company, CBS, that pulled out all the stops. Among the hype was a special report by Paul Gambaccini on his Channel 4 show, *The Other Side Of The Tracks*. It had been a similar Gambaccini report, two years previously, that first brought Kajagoogoo to the attention of the general public. This time, however, it all came to nothing. The

Roaring Boys' debut single took two weeks to clamber to the dizzy heights of number 139 in the charts and then dropped straight back out again. The fans weren't having any of it.

The arrogant assertion that pop fans are being conned is as old as pop itself. Back in 1964, Paul Johnson – then of the *New Statesman*, these days a sycophantic Thatcherite – sneeringly dismissed Beatles' fans in comparison with his own, doubtless rather lofty, experience as a 16-year-old Beethoven devotee. These days it's more likely to be some wiggy German experimentalists or a soul singer the rock critics have just 'discovered' who is held up as offering the authentic aesthetic experience. But the argument is as asinine as it ever was. Not only do the 15- and 16-year-old girls who scream and swoon at Cliff Richard, the Beatles, Marc Bolan, the Osmonds, the Bay City Rollers, Duran Duran, Wham! or Culture Club do so because they enjoy it, they are also taking something very valuable away with them.

At one of Duran Duran's five Wembley Arena concerts at Christmas 1983, I stood on a balcony and watched the fans milling about on the main floor below. At least, it seemed to be milling about. After a minute or two I realized there was a purpose to it all. Gangs of girls were organizing themselves into formations to beat the bouncers. Long before the band appeared, they were standing in groups, chanting and waving and taunting the security guards and having a whale of a time just being there, together, and feeling the power of their collectivity.

Pop writer Sheryl Garratt in her and Sue Steward's book, *Signed Sealed And Delivered*, wrote about the experience of being a Bay City Rollers fan.

'We were a gang of girls having fun together, able to identify each other by tartan scarves and badges. Women are in the minority on demonstrations, in union meetings, or in the crowd at football matches: at the concerts, many were experiencing mass power for the first and last time. Looking back now, I hardly remember the gigs themselves, the songs, or even what the Rollers looked like. What I *do* remember are the bus rides, running home from school together to watch *Shang-A-Lang* on TV, dancing in lines at the school disco and sitting in each others' bedrooms discussing our fantasies and compiling our scrapbooks. Our real obsession was with ourselves; in the end, the actual men behind the posters had very little to do with it at all.'

In the classic model, of which both the Rollers and Duran Duran are prime examples, what the actual men behind the posters *do* have to do with it involves a convoluted process of both desire and identification. Sure, the fans drool over the man of their dreams. But as long as he's a cut-out-and-keep graven image rather than an actual flesh and blood presence, in their dreams is precisely where he remains. This distance is undoubtedly part of the attraction. It's safe. It allows an outlet for all the fans' newly-discovered sexual energy while at the same time allowing them to cling a little longer on to an ideal of romance and true love. Sooner or later the stark realities of burgeoning adulthood will come creeping in, but for the time being, a poster does fine.

And identification? It has often been observed that your average teen idol – Bowie, Bolan, the Sweet, Adam Ant, Limahl, Boy George, Nick Rhodes – is a pretty camp sort of chap, on stage if not elsewhere. Many are openly gay or bisexual. As Simon Napier-Bell noted about Wham!, their buddy-boy act has a definite homo-erotic appeal. Just about every pop star you can name is pretty and vulnerable-looking rather than butch and aggressively masculine. There are lots of reasons why teenage girls might find this type of man attractive. They're safe and unthreatening while at the same time being deviant enough to annoy your average parent. But it's worth noting the way boys, like our Status Quo superfan, identify with 'real men'. By the same token, in the absence of many available female role models, it could be that these feminine boys are the next best thing. Which goes some way to explaining all the imitating of clothes and copying of hair-dos.

George, with all his clone fans, is, of course, an extreme example of all this. But in many ways he's completely different from the classic teen idol. Most pop stars go out of their way to maintain a myth of sexual availability. 'We don't care about looks,' they'll tell the teeny mags, 'it's personality that's important.' This sort of litany is all the more bizarre and hypocritical when intoned by a pop star who is quite clearly either (*a*) gay or (*b*) humping a succession of blonde models.

With George, the personality-not-looks line has considerably more substance. For a start, his sexuality doesn't matter. He's effectively written it out of the equation. No Culture Club fan

expects, even in her wildest dreams, to be carried off and bedded down by Boy George. Jon Moss, maybe, but not George. No, from him they'd expect a cuddle and a nice cup of tea and a chat.

Not so with Duran. On the TV show *Jim'll Fix It*, one fan arranged to have Simon le Bon, dressed as a knight in shining armour, sweep into her classroom, pluck her up and then gallop away with her into the sunset. I'd hazard that approximates the fantasy of just about every girl at that Duran Duran Wembley concert. Sex was in the air. Sex and excitement. A couple of nights later I saw Culture Club at Hammersmith Odeon and the contrast was startling. The atmosphere was completely different: warmer, cosier and a lot less sexual. George, though he does his damnedest to look as glamorous as possible, has always maintained that he is only what he makes of himself, that anyone can make the effort. George speaks to all the fans who are overweight or troubled with acne or otherwise unconfident about their appearance. He tells them they needn't worry about it, that he doesn't care and offers a glittering example of what can be done with some imaginative clothes and a generous dab of make-up. At the end of that concert, he and Helen Terry opened the encore with 'That's The Way (Only Trying To Help You)'. There, on either side of the stage, were this huge great drag queen and this small dumpy woman, two physical misfits singing this tender love song to each other. It moved me to the verge of tears. I've seen them perform it half a dozen times since and it moves me still. Live, it was Culture Club at their best and most effective.

In genuinely discounting the importance of natural, as opposed to carefully constructed, beauty, George gave hope to thousands of potentially insecure teenagers and in doing so revealed himself as a new kind of pop star. From the very first, George has always done his best to reply to as many letters as possible and still makes a hell of an effort. I once conducted an interview with Culture Club based on questions sent in by *Smash Hits* readers. At the end of it, George took the whole sack of mail away with him – hundreds and hundreds of letters – and in time, every single one of them was answered either by him or his mother. On tour in Japan, every morning I'd find Bill Button at the hotel reception, posting a whole pile of letters George had written to fans the night before. Bill reckoned he spent about

£20 or £30 a day on postage. He should know. He has to lick all the stamps.

On the train one day, George showed me a letter he'd had translated into Japanese to send to a fan in Tokyo. 'She said she didn't want to be what her mother wanted her to be,' he explained, 'and I wrote to her and told her that when she's a bit older she'll be able to make that choice for herself. I think it's nice. I'm kind of like a rock and roll social worker. I haven't got the answer but I can offer an example to people to take from. I don't think you ever have the answer but in learning you can help other people. Do you know what I mean?'

I nodded. I do.

'I think I help people in little ways, in the best way I can.'

JAPAN

Through the lamp-lit back-streets of Nagoya, Japan's third city, the Culture Club convoy snakes its way home at exhilarating if not actually dangerous speed. Back at the International Exhibition Hall, the cheering hasn't even died down yet, but already we're half-way back to the hotel. Such manoeuvring is organized with precision: tour manager Gary Lee bawling a Bilko-fashion 'Hup-hup-hup-hup-HUP!' as he herds everyone off the stage, out of the hall and into a waiting line of already revved-up cars; the drivers conferring in feverish Japanese down walkie-talkies as we zoom through tunnels and career around corners. But even this wasn't quick enough to stop about twenty also revved-up cabs full of waiting fans from following in our wake. Nagoya is renowned for this. It's a local sport. The cab drivers who work the beat round the concert hall must all be black-belt pop star-chasers by now.

In a car with trumpeter Ron Williams and photographer André Csillag, I'm right behind the small mini-van that conveys Jon, George, Roy and Mikey. It's exciting. Like a Hollywood car chase without the bullets. Suddenly, out of nowhere, with about half-a-dozen fans crammed in the back seat and urging their driver on to ever more reckless feats of derring-do, a cab swerves hazardously out in front of the pack and matches speed with the van. The fans stretch out of the windows, laughing and shouting and waving and screaming. George laughs and waves back, throwing towels across the gap as the convoy bumps over a bridge and back into town.

'I can't see what anyone could possibly get out of sitting there trying to be the Queen,' George comments over dinner later. 'If I see fans screaming I just want to give them something. You've got to respond and they love it when you do. How can you not be excited by it?'

I've seen Duran Duran fans in Sydney, clutching the usual bulging scrapbooks and hanging around day and night outside the group's apartments, studios, rehearsal hall, etc. I've seen Duran fans in New York, blocking the sidewalk outside the Berkshire Place hotel on 52nd Street, running down the middle of Madison Avenue after limos containing John or Nick or Andy. I've seen John Taylor-trilbied hordes, waving banners as they scream and stream into Madison Square Gardens, or Wembley Arena. I've seen Culture Club fans popping up all over Japan, mobbing Roy and Mikey in the car park of Ryonaji Temple in Kyoto, chasing after Helen Terry in the chic Tokyo district of Harajuku. I've seen so many Japanese Girl Georges riding up and down in hotel lifts looking for the group that I've given up and used the stairs instead. I've seen fifty eager German schoolkids trap Paul Young in the only café open to coach parties on the transit road through East Germany to Berlin. I've even seen Boy George get mobbed by autograph hunters in the middle of an Austrian forest.

I've seen nothing, probably. But it always strikes me as curious how perfectly the form of the New Pop event reproduces itself around the world. There are local variants, sure. American fans can be hard and cynical, offer to suck a pop star's dick before they even say hello. Japanese fans pant and quiver and burst into tears if the same star so much as looks at them. But really, fans – like the groups they follow – look and act the same wherever they are.

In Japan, as Culture Club toured the country in June 1984, that at first seemed to me ridiculous. Certainly, the Japanese have adopted a Western veneer in the years since the Second World War. But MacDonalds and golf and whisky and Mickey Mouse and Burberry coats are one thing. A six-foot soul-singing drag act with ribbons in his hair and rouge on his cheeks I imagined, naïvely, to be another. How on earth did Culture Club get to be the most popular British group in Japan? What the hell do they make of George?

In order to try and figure this out, I began – with the help of Japanese photographer Herbie Yamaguchi – interviewing the fans who milled about the hotel lobbies in Osaka and Nagoya. The replies ranged from the boring ('Boy George is good singer') to the frankly bizarre. ('He has big face.' 'He is like dream.' 'He has eyes of cat.') Many tell me that the lyrics of Western pop – they translate them themselves with dictionaries – are 'deeper' than those of Japanese pop songs. This went not just for Culture Club, but also for Duran, Thompson Twins, Siouxsie and the Cure – other groups that fans mentioned. Several told me that George had given them courage to 'be themselves'. In a country where, as the proverb says, 'a nail that sticks out must be hammered in', a country where the pressure to conform at least outwardly to fixed rules of social conduct is far more relentless than anywhere in the West, a country where an individualist is regarded as a 'crazy', that's no mean feat, if true.

Another common comment was: 'Boy George treats Japan well'. That is to say, he is respectful of and interested in Japanese culture. 'We appreciate that he likes Kyoto,' one fan told me. As the old capital of Japan and the main resting-place of traditional culture amid the onslaught of technology and Westernization, Kyoto is an important symbol for the Japanese.

For his part, George has often used Japanese style on stage, in public and in videos. For that tour of Japan, he used a dress modelled on a Japanese bridal dress for the encore, a mask from the ancient Kabuki theatre for 'Church Of The Poison Mind'. The Kabuki has a long tradition of female impersonation: the *onnagata*. The *onnagata* does not attempt to impersonate a specific woman so much as represent an idealized version of Woman. Yoshisawa Ayame, seventeenth-century master of the art, wrote: 'If an actress were to appear on stage she could not express ideal feminine beauty, for she could only rely on the exploitation of her physical characteristics, and therefore not express the synthetic ideal. The ideal woman can only be expressed by an actor.'

The artifice is precisely the attraction and the tradition continues to this day. Girls' comics are full of androgynous young heroes, called *bishonen*. In a Japanese women's magazine poll, the two 'sexiest stars' of 1981 were Tamasaburo, a Kabuki star specializing in female roles, and Sawada Kenji, a sort of semi-drag pop star. In this context, someone like George has almost more of a footing in Japanese culture than he does in the West. But in Japan, female (or male) impersonation is never a send-up or a caricature. It's deadly serious and regarded as very beautiful. In the West, drag might conjure up images of pantomime dames, Danny La Rue or Barry Humphries' Dame Edna Everage. In Japan it evokes something very much older and deeper.

'He has the power of magic,' one fan, clad in a perfect copy of George's vaguely Japanese outfit from the cover of the 'It's A Miracle/Miss Me Blind' 12-inch, told me, 'Extraordinary power. Boy George is myself.'

'It's funny,' George mused in the van on the way to the concert at Nagoya. 'I'm taking their own ideas and giving them back.' He seems both proud and puzzled by the thought. And sure enough, at that concert, as at others, the audience includes many girls in traditional *geisha* outfits. Girls who, without a kimono-clad George to copy, would probably be wearing trendy Western clothes like everyone else.

In a small dining-room at the Royal Garden Hotel, Hong Kong, the Culture Club entourage are sitting down to a large and lavish meal. The host is Klaus Heymann, the head of Pacific Operations Ltd – the company which licenses Culture Club's records in Hong Kong – and he's hoping to use the occasion to present the group with gold discs for their sales in the territory. Some hope. Roy is the only band member to turn up. Mikey, as usual, has gone straight off to bed. George, it is whispered, was last seen swearing his head off and chasing Jon down the corridor with a bottle in his hand. The gold discs remain in their carrier bags all evening. For the head of Pacific Operations, this compounds an insult he's already received. Tony Gordon – Culture Club's ever thrifty manager – had wired through and asked him to pick up the group's hotel bill. Pacific Operations were not amused. If the group were doing something in Hong Kong, fine. But picking up the tab for a stopover on the way to Japan? What a nerve.

The following morning, Mr Pacific Operations is waiting at the airport, carrier bags full of gold discs in his hands, still hoping for a chance to present them. Still no chance. The group have decided to get a later flight. Only the scum and hangers-on are on this one. He watches, sadly, as we pass into the departure lounge, his carrier bags clutched to his chest.

He never did get to present them. 'There wasn't time,' shrugs Jon, who clearly couldn't care less. When you've already got platinum discs for just about everywhere in the world, including a monstrous great thing for the biggest-selling LP in Canada ever, a couple more for a few thousand sales in Hong Kong are only going to clutter up the place. Not that that makes Mr Pacific Operations any happier.

On the flight, I try and strike up a conversation with Ron Williams, the trumpeter. A Hindu from Portsmouth who'll spend most of the tour locked up in his room doing whatever Hindus do, he's cagier than a politician when confronted with a gentleman of the press. 'I haven't seen Jon Moss for weeks,' he remarks at one point. 'Oh? Haven't you been rehearsing, then?' I enquire innocently. 'No comment, no comment,' Ron splutters. 'No comment.'

The next morning, wandering about Tokyo's Keio Plaza Hotel – a 1500-room establishment with all the charm and atmosphere of a sanatorium for the terminally sick – I catch my first glimpse of George, scuttling about in a kimono at the other end of a corridor. 'Is that Dave Rimmer?' he shouts. 'Hello, Dave.' By the lift, George's assistant Bill Button – 'The man,' as the *Sunday People* will describe him, 'with a beergut of gold' – is having an argument with Gary Lee.

'George wants to go to Kansai.'

'Why there?' Gary Lee, worried about the morning's press conference, wants to know.

'I don't know,' replies Bill firmly, 'but that's where he wants to go.'

Five minutes later, Jon rings down to my room and invites me up to their suite for breakfast. While George is out shopping for clothes, he, still in his dressing gown, is trying to pack. 'Scoop!' he announces as I stroll through the door. 'We haven't rehearsed.' He doesn't seem too worried about it. 'We've played this set, oh, maybe 400 times.' His optimism is maybe a little misplaced.

Everyone else seems to be worried sick and matters aren't helped by *The Tube* filming all through the one afternoon's rehearsal they *do* manage in Osaka. Their first performance of the tour will be distinctly rusty.

At the press conference, in the Capitol Tokyu Hotel and right next to a 'Frozen Yoghurt Festival', the place is buzzing well before the group arrive. 'If any English journalist asks a question,' warns a press officer, 'they'll get thrown out.' Apparently the Japanese aren't used to press conferences and the PR people are worried that English journalists, who are beginning to show up, uninvited, in increasing numbers, will scare them off. The other talking point is the 40,000 handbills for the LP and video that have been printed with the mis-spelling 'Michael Claig'. Nearby, stands a photographer with a 'Fripper The Dolphin' T-shirt.

Roy, Mikey and Jon arrive, but no George. He's still out spending two million yen – about £6500 – on a dress at Kansai. 'Christ,' says Helen Terry when she hears this, 'that's more than some people earn in a year. You could buy a house in Leeds for that.' From then on, George's new dress – which turns out to be too small for him anyway – is always referred to as his 'house in Leeds'.

Whatever, George is late. In Japan this is an unpardonable breach of etiquette and the Virgin press people, who've gone to great lengths to assemble the Japanese media, are worried sick about it. Without George, the conference stumbles along. None of the reporters seem to have anything to ask Jon, Roy or Mikey. After a long, tense silence, someone solicits an opinion about Japanese girls.

'Well . . .' Mikey tries to answer. 'I suppose they're very nice. I've never really experienced girls in Japan. Honestly.'

Another long silence. Someone asks what they think of Duran Duran. 'They're slagged off and you're not. Why is this?'

'That's just the way it is, mate,' Jon snaps in a cockney accent. 'Duran Duran reflect what people can't have in life. We reflect what they *can* have.'

More nervous silence, broken by Jon calling: 'Is Gary Lee about? I think I left my watch in the hotel.'

A few photographers snap away and the questions dry up completely. Then, just as the embarrassment reaches breaking point, George breezes in. From here on, the questions rattle away as fast as the translation back and forth will allow.

What does George think about his popularity?

'There's still a lot of work to be done before it's accepted that what I do is perfectly normal.'

His favourite bands?

'The Smiths.'

No one has heard of them. What does he do with his money?

'I invest it in Culture Club.'

He doesn't mention his house in Leeds.

At the end, which is a relief, each of them is asked to give a message to the press and a message to their fans.

'Dear press people,' says Jon, clearly a little irked by their reception earlier, 'we have far bigger brains than you think we have. You *can* ask us deep and meaningful questions and we *will* answer them.'

Roy: 'Being the philosopher of the band, I'd like to say [*silly high-pitched voice*]: nyik-nyik-nyik-nyik!'

George roars with laughter. 'Is that to the press or to fans?'

Roy: 'Both.'

The next day's papers all comment on George's lateness, but put it down to 'cultural difference'.

At the Taiko-En Garden Restaurant in Osaka the following afternoon, 'cultural difference' is once more a burning issue. 'They said they come at three o'clock,' the manager furrows his brow and peers closely at his watch. It's twenty past. No sign of Culture Club. No sign of the British camera crew from *The Tube* who have hired his establishment to film some interviews. 'Why they not here?' He stares at his watch again, not so much annoyed as apparently unable to understand how this can possibly have happened. The poor chap is so agitated, I rack my brains for some words of comfort but can only come up with a weak shrug and an 'I'm sure they'll be here in a minute.'

Mercifully, they are.

The Taiko-En is a beautiful landscaped garden, with waterfalls, carp-filled streams, wooden bridges and so forth all adding up to another 'synthetic ideal'. It's a peaceful spot. Or at least it would be if there weren't a Geordie film crew of thirteen, a couple of journalists, a couple of photographers, several record company people, a brace of bodyguards and a pop group all milling about in their stockinged feet. Mikey gets a quick shave from Alison Hay. George perches on a stone, dangling his feet in the water and watching the carp swimming up to nibble.

'There's one,' cries Gary Lee excitedly.

'I've seen it,' sniffs George, whipping his foot out of the way. 'They're *repulsive.*'

Bill Button has spent all morning combing the stores of Japan's second largest city for some red hair dye. Did he get it? He shakes his head sadly. Every day Bill has some daft errand to run. Tomorrow he'll be chasing all over after curling tongs. Jon surfaces from the bushes having just completed his interview. He's wearing a curious one-piece striped affair that looks, I suggest, rather like a bathing suit from a Charlie Chaplin film.

'Don't say that,' he grimaces. 'I've got to wear the fucking thing.'

The purpose of the outfit is revealed that night at the Osaka Castle Sports Hall, a spanking new 9000-seater venue that was opened by Duran Duran when their world tour passed this way at the end of 1983. After half an hour's 'cultural difference', in an atmosphere of breathless anticipation punctuated by expectant screams and great sighs of disappointment, the first show of the tour cranks unsteadily into life. It is, as I said, a notably below par performance, but they get away with it. The fans clap in time (or try to, at least – a natural sense of rhythm is not something with which, in all honesty, one could credit the Japanese) right from the opening bars of 'Take Control' through to the dying chords of 'Melting Pot'. They even clap through ballads like 'Black Money' and 'Victims', all the while remaining obediently rooted to their seats. They don't even so much as step out into the aisle. The mild-looking bouncers – each with the cub scout style motto, 'We Do Our Best', emblazoned in English on their T-shirts – don't have to lift a finger. A good old British stage invasion would look to be unthinkable.

To give Fleet Street something to write home about, George appears in his bridal dress and then strips the outer garments from Jon and Mikey to reveal the identical striped Charlie Chaplin bathing suits beneath. These are embellished with what the *Sun* next day refers to as 'skin-coloured cod-pieces'.

'It's not *my* skin colour,' grunts Mikey.

'I like the air of respect around here,' says Jon. 'You don't have to shout your head off to be noticed. I was really looking forward to coming here. I might even come and live here sometime.'

Japanese politeness is something that all of the group note approvingly. Possibly, as jolly famous pop stars, they feel that a humble attitude and an air of respect is nothing less than their due. After a while, though, it can seem oppresive. There is clearly so much bubbling under the surface. In Japan, all conflicts and disagreements are masked by a blank wall of politeness. Even a total contradiction is begun with a, 'Yes, I completely agree with you, but . . .' Here, as with the 'synthetic ideal', the façade is all-important. Pretence is an essential condition of life. Fail to play the game and you'll be excluded from it. All foreigners are excluded anyway, but for a Japanese, it's a fate worse than death. The Japanese have a word for this: *tatemae*. It means the correct public posture, the way things ought to be. The opposite is *honne:* the private feeling or opinion which, most of the time, remains hidden or suppressed. The art of Japanese communication lies in being able to read the *honne* while all the time sticking to the rigid rules of *tatemae.* To the Westerner, this can be intensely irritating. You never know what anyone really thinks, whether anyone really agrees with you or not – a matter complicated somewhat by the fact that Japanese will invariably say 'yes' when they mean 'no' and will usually say 'maybe' when they mean 'yes'. Meanwhile, they probably find Western bluntness and inability to pick up on the delicate subtleties of their *haragei* – 'belly language' – intensely irritating too.

When the code of politeness breaks down, which it does from time to time, the results are startling. The night after the first Osaka concert, Roy and I are treated to a graphic illustration of this.

After only a few days on tour, Roy is already sick to death of being confined to quarters in the hotel and we decide to get out somewhere to do an interview. Accompanied by a couple of security blokes from Udo, the Japanese promoter, we sneak downstairs and steal through the kitchens in order to avoid all the fans in the lobby. It doesn't work. As soon as we're out of the back door we get surrounded by a whole bunch of them. They crowd eagerly around, fetching me a hefty kick in the ankle and clamouring to get at Roy. For the first time, I hear a curious noise that by the end of the tour I'll be well used to. It's a strange panting sound. *Uuuuh! Uuuuh!* An inwardly drawn breath voiced with quivering excitement that Japanese fans emit whenever in close proximity to anyone famous.

'*Uuuuh! Uuuuh!* Roy-ee! Roy-ee!' they all shout, running along behind as the security guards herd us in the direction of the nearest restaurant. '*Uuuuh! Uuuuh!*'s and 'Roy-ee's continue outside most of the time we're in there. They peer through the window and try to attract Roy's attention – 'Roy-ee! Roy-ee!' – until the owner shuts the blinds.

An hour or so later, our conversation is winding down and a drunken salaryman comes over to ask for an autograph. 'Hoko,' he says, presenting a square of stiff white card that all Japanese seem to have handy for this very contingency. 'H-O-K-O . . .' Roy signs. As we continue talking, Hoko, so drunk he's reeling, gets into an argument with one of our security guys. They'd told him to wait until we'd finished and are annoyed that he didn't. In a second, Hoko, the guards and the owner of the restaurant are all shoving and shouting and holding each other back.

'Oh dear, this is so horrible,' Roy murmurs as Hoko is bundled out of the door and comes staggering back in again, shouting and waving his arms. 'Don't hit him . . .'

It takes about ten minutes for everyone to calm down again. Hoko wanders over, bows and shakes both of our hands. 'Nice to meet you,' he smiles apologetically and points to himself. 'Crazy Japanese . . .' The restaurant owner is mortified. As we get up to leave, he bows low, wrings his hands and mumbles feverish apologies. Roy and I, as embarrassed as he is, start bowing too. For about a minute, the three of us stand there, bobbing up and down in a furious affirmation that politeness reigns once more.

The hotel lobby is full of fans. They sit quietly all morning, trying to blend in with the background. Some of them explain that they've left their clone gear elsewhere in the hope the hotel authorities won't realize what they are. But as soon as Jon or George move through, they erupt in a frenzy of *Uuuuh! Uuuuh!*s and all whip out their white autograph cards. In the ensuing chaos, they even begin asking *me* for my autograph. From time to time, a pair of fans will wander quietly up, wondering whether I'm one of the group. 'Are you keyboard player?' asks one. I shake my head. 'Are you trumpeter?'

Oddest of all is the rumour that apparently runs round the crowd in the Keio Plaza lobby when we return to Tokyo. It seems they suspect that *I'm* George, minus wig, drag or make-up. Whenever I walk through, heads turn, eyes follow and the odd fan runs shyly up.

Before the second Osaka concert, I wander over to look at the castle with press officer Ronnie Gurr. Tagging along is John Blake, then of the *Sun*, these days of the *Daily Mirror*. Britain's most notorious pop writer and responsible for the historic 'Culture

Club To Split' gaffe among many others, Blake is here without official sanction, just trying to pick up what he can. Ronnie, having promised Fleet Street exclusives elsewhere, is busy making sure this is as little as possible.

The result has been a series of rows with manager Tony Gordon, who is labouring under the twin misapprehensions that (*a*) John Blake is a nice bloke and (*b*) any publicity is good publicity. A curious phenomenon, Tony Gordon. He is someone of whom I have never heard anyone, ever – with the exception of George, Jon, Roy and Mikey – utter an even remotely kind word. On tour, accompanied by his wife, Avie, he appears to be spending his entire time eating, having massages in his lavish suite and sticking his nose into the business of various perfectly competent record company people. They moan about it incessantly. 'Have you heard what Tony Gordon's gone and done *now*?' becomes a familiar, long-suffering refrain. No one can understand why he's not off somewhere, you know, *managing* the group. On tour, there are people called tour managers who are supposed to take care of things. Not that Gary Lee seems to have a very firm grip on anything either.

Anyway, Tony Gordon keeps telling Ronnie he is being 'too rude' to Fleet Street. Ronnie, on the other hand, the man who steered Culture Club's press with a firm hand from the very beginnings of the group, is getting well fed up with Gordon telling him how to do his job. Two days later, Ronnie resigns in disgust and flies back to Britain. The group try to make out that they have sacked him. I'd arrived in Japan thinking Culture Club were a damn near perfect pop group. Now, seeing how shabbily they treat many of those who work for them, I'm beginning to have my doubts.

Meanwhile, John Blake, ever so delicately, is trying to pump me for information. 'What does George think about Pete Burns?' he'll ask nonchalantly. 'What does he think about Frankie?' 'Oh, I don't know,' I reply, pretending I don't know Blake hasn't an interview of his own. 'Why don't you ask him?'

Around the back of the Sports Hall, we stop to talk to a group of fans clustered around a banner that reads: 'We ♥ Coulture Club!' They want to know what I'm doing here, so I mime a typewriter and mention *Smash Hits*. 'Ah! *Smashitsu!*' one exclaims, and all burst into a round of applause and a chorus of

'*Uuuuh! Uuuuh!*'s. There's a telephone box nearby and Blake has chosen this moment to try and phone the *Sun*. He emerges, unsuccessful. 'All I got was some little Nippy voice,' he sniffs. The fans have been in a huddle. Now they turn round and all begin chanting: 'We want to go to Rondon! We want to go to Rondon!' The phone rings in the box. I pick it up and am greeted with a recorded American voice talking about Father's Day: 'A typical father is strong, self-willed, he *cares* for his children . . .' Hurriedly, I put the phone down again. 'We want to go to Rondon! We want to go to Rondon!' The phone rings again. 'Did you send *your* father a card on Father's Day?' Badly shaken, I slam it back down. 'WE WANT TO GO TO RONDON! WE WANT TO GO TO RONDON! *Uuuuh! Uuuuh! Uuuuh!*'

Right then, a small mini-van bearing the group comes hurtling down the road. 'Rimme-e-e-er!' taunts Roy from behind a curtain as it careers round the corner and towards the stage door. The fans, on the look-out for a lavish limo and 'Uuuuh!'-ing and chanting out their desire to visit the United Kingdom, don't even notice.

And then the phone rings again.

The coach bearing all of the Culture Club entourage bar Jon and George – they're off in a car having pictures taken somewhere – pulls out of Osaka with the usual fleet of fan-bearing cabs in attendance. Mikey reclines in his seat, plugged into a Walkman. Roy laughs and jokes. 'Who's coming out mole-bashing tonight, then?' *Mogura Tatake* – literally, I think, 'mole-hitting' – is a common Japanese arcade game. Little plastic moles with stupid cross-eyed expressions pop up out of holes and you beat them back down with a mallet. Everyone thinks it's hilarious and 'mole-bashing' becomes tourspeak for going out on the town.

Fifty miles or so later, with no break having yet been spotted in the endless houses and factories, one cab of fans is still on our tail. Matching speed with the coach, they hold up a sign: 'WHERE'S JON?'

'Who cares?' drawls Roy, and then notices me making notes. 'Don't put "Who cares?" He'll kill me. Actually, it does make a change. It's normally "Where's George?" '

Mikey carefully writes out a bold felt-tip reply and holds it up to the window. 'Jon went in car because bus makes him ill.' The fans lean forward intently, trying to decipher this missive. Then nod and wave.

Arriving in Kyoto before we seem to have left the outskirts of Osaka, the coach pulls into the car park of Ryonaji Temple. Scenes of ordinary madness ensue as crowds of uniformed schoolkids all going '*Uuuuh! Uuuuh!*' spot Roy and Mikey and trap them in the coach. One of them passes a note to Roy: 'Do you like girls? I want to sleep beside you.' Alison, reading over his shoulder, mutters brightly: 'his wife ain't going to like it.'

We wander up to look at one of the most famous stone gardens in Japan. Various bits of rock stick up out of a bed of raked pebbles. 'If you stare at it long enough something beautiful is supposed to happen,' reckons Mikey. We stare. Nothing happens. The pebbles, explain photographer Herbie, represent waves or clouds or fluctuations in life. The rocks are islands or mountaintops or major events in a life. Everyone does their best to pretend it's a deeply aesthetic experience.

Back in the coach and round the corner to a restaurant where Mr Udo, the promoter, treats us to a traditional *sukiaki* meal: chopsticks, rice paper walls, brimming bowls of *sake*, women in *geisha* gear kneeling and cooking it all up at the table, the works. It's the best Japanese meal I have ever had. Tony Gordon suddenly starts quizzing Mr Udo about the war. Everyone chokes on their bean curd, splutters out their *sake* and exchanges nervous glances across the table, but Udo handles the gaff with unfailing politeness. After the meal, Udo presents the group with beautiful bolts of Japanese silk. Vaguely thinking of buying one for a friend, I enquire after the price. A snip at £700 a throw. My friend gets a kimono instead.

That night Jon and I slip out of the hotel in Nagoya and over the road to an arcade for an hour's mole-bashing and a chat with a local punk. Two of Udo's security guys come too, one holding an umbrella for Jon. The punk is thrilled to meet Jon. He knows all about his time with the Damned, Clash and so forth. Handing Jon a thick black felt-tip, he asks him to autograph his T-shirt.

Jon draws an arrow pointing up to the kid's head, and writes underneath: 'Japan's Number One Punk!' On the way back into the hotel, a few fans crowd round Jon and shower him with presents. One is a box containing a series of smaller boxes, in the last of which is a letter addressed to 'Mr Jon Moss'.

'Oh, that's lovely,' he says. 'You'll have to mention that, Dave. The fans here are so sweet. In America it's horrible, you know. They come up to you and go (*lowers voice*): "Suck your dick?" ' He grimaces. 'It's disgusting.'

I refrain from mentioning that I've a friend who, when she was a teenage fan and Jon was the drummer with London, once had it off with him in a broom cupboard at Middlesbrough Town Hall.

'**G**eorge!' calls Roy impatiently. 'Hup-hup-hup-hup-HUP!' It's well past time to leave for the concert. Jon, Mikey, Helen and all the other musicians have been at Nagoya's International Exhibition Hall for hours, but in his hotel suite, George is still getting ready. Looks like another case of 'cultural difference'.

George's door opens a crack. 'Scisso-o-ors!' he bellows from within. Everyone laughs. The door slams. 'Bill!' relays Tony Gordon. 'Scissors!' Bill Button, former butcher, zooms down the corridor with the desired implements. He knocks gently and passes them in.

'Bill!' George bellows again. 'Bring the curling tongs as well.'

'I've got 'em,' Bill replies calmly. He's used to George shouting at him. 'And he knows I don't mean it,' George tells me later.

At last George appears and hurries into another room to have his picture taken with four local Girl Georges. They're all so consumed with excitement they can scarcely breathe. They cling on to him for dear life and, one by one, all burst into tears. George giggles. 'I'm more nervous than they are, I'm telling you.'

Then we all tumble into the lift, down to the basement, into waiting cars and off to the concert. I'm bundled into the mini-van with Roy, George and Tony Gordon. On the way, I take the piss out of Roy's guitar hero bit during 'Miss Me Blind'.

'I like the guitar now but I used to hate it,' comments George. 'I didn't want him to do it on the record and then they went and did it while I was off for an afternoon at the dentist's or something and when I came back I wanted to say I didn't like it but I did.'

'Well that was nice, wasn't it?' says Tony Gordon when we arrive at the hall. 'What a nice chat.' 'Nice' is Tony's favourite word. He wants everything to be nice. No arguments, no fuss. Just an awful lot of niceness.

Backstage, Jon tells me of a nightmare he'd had after our mole-bashing session. He dreamt that he was having dinner with Richard Branson and Simon Draper – respectively owner and managing director of Virgin Records. In the dream, Branson was twelve-years-old and couldn't stop crying. Jon, feeling sorry for him, put his arm round Branson's shoulders and started sobbing too. 'Don't worry Richard,' he crooned, stroking his hair. 'It'll be all right.' Then he dreamt that he'd bought a council flat on a rough London estate. There was a fascist march outside and skinheads all dressed in red started pushing him around. He ran away and hid in a basement, looking around for weapons.

George appears from his dressing-room, dances around in front of me and hitches up his skirt. 'Look' he grins, 'freshly-Immaced legs.' Roy sits picking out the *Crossroads* theme on his guitar.

'Come on!' bawls Gary Lee. 'The quicker we can get on stage the quicker we can all get out mole-bashing!'

After the two dodgy Osaka performances, tonight it all comes together: a brisk, uplifting show in front of 10,000 fans who, needless to say, clap through everything including 'Victims'. For the first time, the group really seem to be enjoying themselves on stage. The only hitch is George's *Kabuki* mask. In the long intro to 'Church Of The Poison Mind', while Helen briefly takes centre stage, George rushed off to change as usual. Coming back, a little late, he suddenly realizes the mask isn't on properly and that he can't sing through it. He pauses in the wings, pushes it back, composes himself and dashes on stage. After the song he ducks back offstage and angrily tries to rip the mask off. After a lot of tugging, it comes loose eventually. Worried that he's smudged his eyebrows, he shouts at Bill Button to get him a mirror, then dives back on stage for 'Victims'. Bill readies himself with a torch and a mirror and George rushes straight back to check his make-up. It's fine. And even if it hadn't been, only about two dozen of the 10,000 out front could possibly have noticed. George won't wear the mask again, though. For the remaining three concerts at the Tokyo Budokan, the old *Colour By Numbers* bedspread outfit comes out of mothballs to take its place.

That night I have dinner with George. He's in a good mood but lectures me about how he only trusts me because Jon Moss thinks I'm OK. I'm not sure how to react to this but I know what to say when everyone else leaves and Tony Gordon wanders up and says: 'I've paid for your dinner, Rimmer. Make it a good article.'

'It'll take more than a meal to buy me, dear,' I snap back.

Five minutes later, Tony Gordon and Avie are back, having investigated the road crew party upstairs and found it to be 'not very nice'. They order coffee and he calls over to the table where George and I are still talking: 'You'll pay for this, won't you, Dave?' Coming from a multi-millionaire, I take this to be a joke and promptly forget about it.

As we all walk out of the restaurant a little later, a waiter goes rushing up to Tony Gordon with a bill. 'Oh, he'll take care of that,' he points at me, disappearing downstairs and leaving me to fumble, embarrassed, for my wallet.

I look in on the road crew party. Everyone, bar George, Tony Gordon and Avie, is up there. Mikey is at one table surrounded by fans. Phil Pickett is at the piano with Steve Grainger and Ron Williams playing sax and trumpet in an impromptu version of 'Knees Up, Mother Brown'. I arrive at the bar just as Roy turns away from it with a trayful of drinks. 'He'll pay,' he calls to the barman, jerking a finger at me. This *is* a joke, but I just stalk off to bed.

The next morning, on the train, George is in a furious temper. He stomps around and mutters darkly about people who work for *him* exploiting *his* popularity to get off with *his* fans. Everyone keeps out of his way. 'Sometimes I wonder what I'm doing in this group,' he glares around him. 'I've got nothing in common with any of them.'

131

'**I**'m really fucking pissed off and you can quote me on that,' announces Jon when I bump into him one morning back at the Keio Plaza. He prowls around the forty-first floor, staring out of windows at the city spread below him, wishing he could get out and about without a phalanx of security guards for company. 'I hate touring. It's so brainless. You just get bored. Even if you partied every night you'd still get bored.'

Roy feels the same way. He and Alison wander around every night from one of the hotel's many bars to another, all dressed up with nowhere to go. Mikey doesn't comment, but seems to get out a bit more. The only one who doesn't mind the confinement is George. He potters about in the suite he shares with Jon, writing letters and making clothes and working on his book.

'One of the papers said what a sad existence I must have, that I don't have a social life,' he says. 'But I do have a social life. Our floor in the hotel is like a little street in suburbia. We all pop in to see each other and have a cup of tea.' Which, of course, is better than sex. 'It's just like when I was living in a squat, only now I make a lot more money.'

Helen Terry and saxophonist Steve Grainger, on the other hand, go mole-bashing whenever the opportunity presents itself. Most nights, in other words. They're usually joined by various other members of the entourage. Like me. One night, Helen and I end up in a *karaoke* bar – a place where customers can choose from a menu of songs and get up and croon to a backing track. We watch a crowd of dark-suited salarymen, the cares of the day being washed away by the attention of hostesses and large quantities of Suntory whisky, happily singing their hearts out. One comes over. 'You know Harrod's department store?' We nod. 'I install computer in Harrod's department store,' he announces proudly, then grabs my arm. 'You sing.' I try to get out of it, but Helen eggs him on and he literally drags me out of my seat. In the end, I croak my way through 'Yesterday' – the only English song they can find – and the whole place erupts: normally polite businessmen shouting and whistling and banging on tables.

I try and get Helen to sing something, but she refuses point blank. 'I can do it in front of 10,000 people, but I can't in front of ten.'

In the Presidential Suite, George is organizing a photo session. Herbie Yamaguchi, who's known George since the Warren Street squat days, is being ordered about a lot.

'Get some coffee.'

'Fetch me my make-up box.'

'Get a mirror.'

'Where from?' Herbie wonders.

'I don't know,' George rages. 'Anywhere. There's about a thousand people working for us, someone must be able to get me a mirror.' He pauses. 'If Gary Lee can arrange women for people I'm sure he can arrange a mirror.'

Two minutes later, Herbie returns with one. George is storming around. 'Where's the band?' he shouts into the corridor. 'Roy! Jon! Mikey! Where are you? Someone find the band. This isn't a holiday, you know.'

Jon's in the next room, telling me what's on the tape he uses on stage. George overhears and shouts through: 'Don't tell him that! We're not the Thompson Twins!'

Jon raises his eyes to heaven. 'He knows that.'

A little later, the photo session is in full swing. 'Mikey,' orders George, 'go and put your other outfit on.' He means the Charlie Chaplin thing.

'Look,' replies Mikey, 'I've had photos in the yellow outfit. I've had photos in the black outfit. There are backstage photos in the other outfit.'

'But the backstage ones are awful. I want a photo done here with the studio lights.'

Mikey just shakes his head.

'Well if you look ugly in the photos,' shouts George, 'don't come complaining to me.'

'I always look ugly in the photos you choose anyway so what does it matter?' And with that, Mikey storms out.

In the course of this altercation, Jon, a flower in one hand and a doll in the other, has been advancing step by step across the room towards me. He holds the flower out, smiles and says: 'Good!' He takes a step forward, hunches round the doll, pulls a face and says: 'Evil!' Flower out again: 'Good!' Then the doll: 'Evil!'

George shouts over at him: 'Jon, go and get Tony to make him put it on.'

'I'm not going to make him put it on,' protests Jon.

'I didn't say that,' seethes George through clenched teeth. 'I said get Tony to make him put it on.'

Jon drops both flower and doll, strides towards the door and declaims in the voice of a small child telling tales: 'Toneee! Toneee! Make Mikey put his Kansai top on!'

Everyone giggles. George storms out, slams the door, thumps Jon and stalks the corridor scowling: 'No one round here wants to do *anything!*'

Later on, George draws me aside and gives me another lecture. 'If you print anything about that I'll be really annoyed,' he says. 'In print these arguments look a lot more serious than they really are. The thing is, they're forgotten ten minutes later.'

Or are they? 'I'd like to think of Culture Club as an example to the world,' Mikey tells me one night. 'I'm Black, Jon is Jewish, George is Irish and Roy is English. I'd like the world to look at that and say: "This is how it should be." But even with us it gets difficult sometimes. Each of us has an ego. We all want to be the leader and we all want to be first. That frightens me an awful lot. It keeps us thriving, because that's the way the Western world works, but it frightens me a lot.'

Tokyo's Budokan, built in 1964 for the Tokyo Olympics, is a vast place with a huge domed ceiling. Nevertheless, on Culture Club's third and final night, the 12,000 crowd more than fills the place. Helen declares it to be 'the largest sauna in the world'. In fact, Budokan means 'House of Martial Arts'. Backstage, there is a *kendo* class going on all through the concert: a crowd of men in robes and masks beating, as one Virgin Records person puts it, 'seven kinds of shit out of each other'.

'Here-we-go-again-oh-my-god-it's-so-boring,' Jon grins over at me and does a silly, stiff march up the steps and on to the stage. George, as usual, stays behind a few moments to yelp into his radio mike and wind the audience up.

'Yelp!'

The audience answers.

'This is my favourite bit – YELP!'

They all answer again.

'It's brilliant – YELP! YELP!'

Twelve thousand people YELP! YELP! back.

'I think I'll stay here and not even sing a note,' he giggles. 'Stand by the side where I can see you,' he calls as he runs up to join the others. 'It always makes me laugh when I can see someone I know.'

The concert is smooth and exciting, the audience loud and excitable – but not so much so that they get on their seats. That isn't allowed. But by the time it gets to 'Karma Chameleon' there is hysteria in the ranks. Every move of George's raises a scream and hails of bouncy rubber balls are thrown, for some reason, on to the stage.

Backstage before the first encore, Helen is telling Steve Grainger. 'God, I was so bored on stage tonight. I started thinking about my laundry.' This is Helen's last tour with the group and she didn't much want to come in the first place. George persuaded her.

Jon, on the other hand, didn't think about his laundry at all. 'I was really laughing on stage tonight. I don't know why. Just everybody enjoying themselves. We're such an odd bunch on stage. All stumbling around.' He puts a bunch of bananas on his head and dances about. 'Shall I go on like this?' He doesn't.

'I'm going to go back on and wind them up,' announces George and disappears. Sounds of yelping filter back. Roy arrives and laughs. 'Is he on already? What a big 'ead.' Then the rest of the group join him for 'White Boy'.

During the second encore, while Roy, Helen and George do 'That's The Way', Jon and Tony Gordon discuss the logistics of doing Madison Square Gardens in the round on their next American tour. 'We're doing three nights there,' boasts Jon. 'We could do five. We could do two nights at Anaheim. 150,000 people. Ridiculous!'

Ridiculous is precisely what this claim will turn out to be. Meanwhile, the group do their final number, 'Melting Pot', bow, and then belt out the back. 'Hup-hup-hup-hup-HUP!' yells Gary Lee as we all pad up an iron staircase and leap into the waiting cars. I end up with Jon and Roy. This time, as we scoot through the streets, there isn't a convoy at all. Roy seems disappointed. He winds down a window and waves at some fans: 'Hello! Hello!' They don't even notice. There is, however, a huge crowd of them outside the hotel and plenty more lining the tunnel as we twist and turn down into the underground carpark.

Two girls are waiting by the lift in near hysterics, held at bay by two security guards. They screech and wail when they catch sight of George getting out of the van. 'Calm down! Calm down!' he shouts, although it's impossible to tell whether he means the two fans or the over-zealous security guards who are roughly pushing them back. 'Let them through. I'll sign.'

The girls run up, cling on to George and start sobbing their hearts out. 'Calm down,' he says more softly, signing their programmes, kissing their cheeks and shaking their hands.

And then he slips into the lift and is gone.

MONEY

On the last morning in Japan, I felt it was finally time to mention the idea of this book. I hadn't dared bring it up before. George, I reckoned, might just fly off the handle and refuse to talk to me – which is exactly what did happen, in the end. Jon seemed the best bet. The most bookish of the group as well as the most level-headed and the one with the closest eye on business affairs, he was likely to be the most sympathetic and the clearest about the practicalities involved. So I arranged to talk to him 'about some business'.

We did the usual sneaking down service elevators and stealing through laundry rooms and slipped out for a stroll together around Shinjuku. In one of the area's many coffee houses – another import from the West – we talked it over. A serious study of Culture Club, broadening out into a larger picture of British pop in the 1980s? Something done in cooperation with the group but by no means an 'official' biography or anything? Jon thought it sounded like a good idea.

'There's just one thing,' he told me between sips of Blue

Mountain coffee. 'You're going to have to give us a percentage.'
I'd expected this, of course, but made protesting noises.

'Oh, don't worry,' he went on. 'It won't be very much. But the thing with George is, if you don't give him anything he'll think you're ripping him off.'

I was keen to cooperate but it never worked out. Jon suggested that I came to America in autumn 1984. In the meantime he'd talk to the others about it and, when everyone was back in London, I should get in touch with Tony Gordon. So I did. I rang him a couple of times but just got the brush-off from a rather curt secretary who told me they 'weren't planning any books'. I sent a synopsis over by messenger but never got so much as an acknowledgement. The only time I managed to pin Tony Gordon down about it was when one day we both ended up on the same flight to Amsterdam. He could hardly pretend he was in a meeting then. 'We haven't any time now but we will have time in the New Year,' he said in mildly discouraging tone. Time for what? All I needed was an interview or two, an OK to go tag along for a couple of the American concerts as Jon had suggested and an arrangement to give *them* money. Gordon was resolutely non-committal.

And then I saw Jon again. He'd seen the synopsis and thought it 'pretty straightforward' and I wasn't going to dig up any *dirt*, was I? 'Not that there's any dirt to dig up,' he added. The day before they left for their autumn 1984 American tour – with still nothing decided and all journalists banned from the trip – he told me he'd pass the synopsis on to George.

'I can't do any more or he'll think we're in league against him or something,' he said, clearly a bit bored with the subject. Why didn't I just go ahead and do it? 'He'll be angry about it at first but he'll get over it.'

And that was the closest I ever got to an official position.

I don't know whether George ever did see the synopsis, but the next time he saw me – on New Year's Eve – he wouldn't speak to me. By that time I no longer cared. Over a period of months I'd gone out of my way to keep them informed and allow them, if they wanted, to be involved. All I'd got in return were shrugs and evasions. I was going ahead and sod them all.

A pop group makes its money in a number of different ways. There are royalties on record sales, publishing royalties, money from records being played on the radio, revenue from touring and merchandizing and so forth. The New Pop never came up with any new ways of making money. It simply tried to exert an increased vigilance to ensure the largest possible slice of each of those various cakes. That, when you get to the bottom line, is what 'controlling your own destiny' is all about.

But of course, it goes deeper than that.

Take merchandizing. Handled correctly, this is a source of millions. Literally. On their last American tour, The Rolling Stones made five million dollars from T-shirt sales alone. One of the first things Jon Moss does after a Culture Club show is check out the T-shirt sales. A major act like Police actually plans tours according to the ins and outs of T-shirt deals.

'If you play a 13,000-seater hall in somewhere like Tallahassee, Florida,' explains Police manager Miles Copeland, 'they're so glad that you're using their facility that they won't charge any commission on T-shirt sales. But if you play Madison Square Garden the hall can take up to 50 per cent commission so you can end up losing money. It becomes more profitable to play to 13,000 people in Tallahassee than 35,000 people in New York City.

'We're not in the music business anymore. We're in the commodities business.'

Those commodites can be T-shirts, watches, dolls, posters, badges, make-up kits, board games, wigs or books. Anything at all that is endorsed by the group, manufactured under licence and paying them a percentage. Often, merchandizing is sold through fan clubs which, with thousands of committed members, act in this instance as a ready-made mail order outlet. Do your merchandizing properly, and it not only makes money, it also reflects well on you in the eyes of the public. Duran Duran, for instance, keep all their merchandizing under tight artistic and quality control. Everything is designed by the same Assorted iMaGes team who do their record sleeves, tour programmes and so forth. Thus everything, be it LP, book or board game, is recognizably part of the same Duran corporate image and up to a certain standard. If you don't take care of your own merchandizing, then someone else will take care of it for you. The field is full of mavericks. Merchandizing happens despite you, your image is damaged and the fans get royally ripped off.

Poster magazines are a good example. As soon as a group has a couple of hits and proves it has a following, newsstands everywhere suddenly become clogged up with unauthorized and usually rather shoddy poster magazines. In order to try and control this – both for reasons of quality and because it takes sales away from official merchandizing – groups try and throw a copyright net over all photographs that are taken of them. A photographer on assignment, for Fleet Street or the music press, will have to sign a legally-binding form stating that the photos he or she takes are only to be used for such-and-such a purpose. I know of no case where one of these forms has gone to court but few photographers are willing to risk the possible repercussions of breaking these agreements. Only very big groups can get away with this, of course, but all the big groups do it.

The next step is allowing only your own photographer to take pictures of you. David Bowie, Duran Duran and Spandau Ballet all employed Denis O'Regan on their respective world tours. Culture Club use André Csillag. The agreement is that the photographer can do more or less what he or she wants with the pictures – though some control is exerted over their destination – as long as the artist approves the pictures to be used. This means that only photos of the group looking as they want to look are allowed to be published. It also leads to some pretty silly situations. In New York I had to stand and catch each member of Duran Duran in between the hotel lift and the limo that was to take them out of town, hauling them over in turn to the nearest light to get them to approve the transparencies I needed to accompany my story. In Tokyo, I waited two extra days for George to approve a shot for the cover of *Smash Hits*. At one point, I was literally *on my knees* in the hotel corridor, begging George to find time to look at the bloody pictures. I flew home right after my conversation with Jon about the book, still without the shot I needed.

Controlling your own destiny. The idea seeps through into everything. It gets ridiculous. Groups want to control it all. The Human League once came into the *Smash Hits* office to raise hell, outraged that we hadn't put them on the cover. Another time they complained vociferously on national radio because they didn't like a shot we *had* used on the cover – one that they'd approved, I might add.

Adam Ant once moaned: 'I pay photographers money – *my* money – to use photographs that they've taken of me at my concerts. They come to my concerts *free* and take pictures and I have to *pay* them to use their pictures of me. Without me going on in the make-up and creating it they wouldn't have anything to film. It's not right.'

Which is as silly as George thinking he's being ripped off if someone writes a book about him and doesn't give him a slice. Not that I would have minded giving Culture Club a piece of this book, because it would have involved some publicity in return. Pop stars *sell* things. That's the point. They've pushed and preened and charmed and sweated their way into the firmament called the star system. Once there, they find that everything they shine on assumes a value. They don't just sell records and concert tickets and T-shirts. They sell newspapers and magazines and books too. And they feel they have a right to a piece of it all.

It's all, in other words, grist to the millions.

The millions start with recording deals. Sure, the money starts flowing in from all over the place once the ball is rolling, but a recording contract is the foundation of it all. Here's how it works.

In business terms, a record is simply a piece of black plastic to be sold in as large a quantity as possible. As with any commodity produced in a capitalist society, the vast majority of people involved in the making and marketing of that piece of black plastic simply get paid a wage or fee for their time. They then have no further economic interest in it and, except for key record company personnel, no say in what happens to it. A piece of black plastic, however, needs an artiste to imbue it with value. Artistic labour is special. Artistes are rewarded with a cut in the final profits because their necessary creative skills would otherwise be difficult for their purchaser to control. Obviously, there are some fine distinctions here. Helen Terry, for example, contributed a hell of a lot to the sound and personality of Culture Club. But, employed as a session musician, she was simply paid a fee for her time and had no stake in the product at all.

143

The cut of final profits is paid as a royalty – a percentage of the price of each record sold. When a group signs with a record company, they are given an advance against future royalties to take care of their personal needs, buy their stage clothes and equipment and pay for the cost of recording songs. This is like an interest-free loan. The artist pays for everything in the end – or else disappears down the dumper and is written off as a bad debt by the company.

An awful lot of artists disappear down the dumper. In 1983, around 6000 singles were released in Britain. Only a tiny fraction of these made it into the charts. An even smaller fraction actually made money, although the break-even point varies enormously from record to record. Despite all the skill and professionalism of the record companies, the pop market remains notoriously difficult to control. The companies are therefore left in the position of throwing a lot of money around in the hope that at least some of it will land with an act who are going to provide a handsome return on their investment. A successful record company needs a large amount of fluid capital for this purpose. It's one of the reasons why independents find it difficult to compete with majors: they can't afford such a low hit-to-release ratio.

While the companies are looking for groups to imbue their bits of black plastic with artistic value, the groups are looking at the companies simply as mechanisms to manufacture and market the product of their artistic labours. Once upon a time, before the Beatles, the record companies called all the shots. They decided what was recorded and how, what was released and when. They paid new groups a very small royalty, subject to later re-negotiation on the basis of proven popularity. In fact, this still goes on, although it's by no means as common as it was.

With the lessons of punk under their belts, the New Pop groups wanted more. In the often correct belief that they knew better than the companies what would sell, they reserved all artistic control to themselves. Often they acted more like packaging companies: taking the company's money, making their records their own way, providing their own artwork and videos and everything, and giving it all back to the company with instructions about the release date. If something went wrong then, as far as they were concerned, it must be the company's fault. Thus, in early 1985, Spandau Ballet – irked that they had not yet broken

144

America – entered into legal action against their record company, Chrysalis, for failing 'to honour its contract and promote the group as agreed'. That the problem could have something to do with their own material – Chrysalis could hardly be accused of failing to promote the international hit 'True', for example – never entered their heads.

As for royalties, these are still in some sense supposed to be an index of popularity. The bigger you are, the bigger a royalty you get – for the simple reason that a company will concede a reduced profit margin on a greater volume of sales. Thus Michael Jackson gets more 'points', as they're called in the business, than anyone else in history. In the post-Sex Pistols era, the trick is to wring as much money as possible out of a record company by establishing a high level of popularity before you've signed a deal or released a record. Here we enter the realm of hype. Hype – a contraction of hyperbole – is the time-honoured art of inflating something beyond its natural proportions through judicious manipulation of publicity. This is done in the hope that a record company, the general public, whoever, believes that whatever you're hyping is as big and important as you make it appear to be. All those early Duran Duran videos in exotic climes were an example of muted hype, making the band out to be massively successful international jet-setters long before they were. Frankie Goes To Hollywood, like the Sex Pistols before them, are flagrant hype from start to finish, which is one of the things that's good about them.

In the period immediately following the new romantics, hyping a group into a deal was as easy as pie. Every record company wanted a piece of the new action, but needed to be told just what that action was. The style pundits decided that Latin would be the Next Big Thing and said so, loud and often. Thus Blue Rondo A La Turk – an Anglo-Latin ensemble who dressed in supposedly hip zoot suits, went through the then usual rigmarole of secret gigs and had a lot of friends who were style pundits – conned their way into an enormous advance from Virgin. Despite all the fashion spreads, name-dropping and magazine covers, their biggest record, 'Me And Mr Sanchez', got no further than number forty.

Even when the hype is backed up by genuine talent, the fashion for vast amounts of money up front seriously affects

145

everything that follows. In order to recoup their investment – and, in the process, satisfy their artistes by making instant stars out of them – companies have to resort to the most aggressive marketing tactics possible. Once that starts, everyone has to follow. In mid-1983, there was a period when those shops whose sales are used to compile the charts were positively flooded with free gifts to be given away with singles – T-shirts, cassettes, even videos. Naturally, this kind of promotion ups the financial ante even further.

As investment rises, so does the break-even point. As the break-even point rises, so does the investment necessary to reach it. In Silicon Valley, they call this 'betting on the upside'. Everything is staked on massive success. Boom or bust. The vicious circle is completed by the high cost of modern recording technology and the time it takes to make a record with it. In 1972, in Michael Wale's *Voxpop*, Joseph Lockwood, then Group President of EMI, moaned that an artist like John Lennon 'could spend, and I know it sounds stupid, they could spend a week on making a single'. These days a record company would regard itself as damn lucky if your average pop group recorded a single in that time. A high-tech perfectionist producer like Trevor Horn can take a hell of a lot longer.

Indeed, Horn and the whole ZTT operation are a classic example of betting on the upside. They use fearfully expensive studios and the very highest-tech of modern recording technology with a whole team of experts *in situ* to operate it. They take, sometimes, literally months to record a single and to top it all off spend a bloody fortune on advertising. Their break-even points are such that it takes nothing less than the kind of success that Frankie Goes To Hollywood have had to get any kind of return on investment. There are ZTT groups who, even after they've had hits, are still getting negative royalty statements. Not that this would worry Trevor Horn. With his wife Jill Sinclair, he runs the show, owns the studios and bosses the label. While he spends two days getting one note right, say, the ever-escalating recording costs which the group are paying go right back through his company. Profits on record sales, studio fees, producer's cut: Trevor Horn wins every way.

Of course, this isn't the only way to work. At the other end of the extreme, you get a performer like Billy Bragg. Although he

146

does a lot of benefits, Bragg can probably now command about a thousand quid a performance. As it's just him and a guitar, it doesn't cost a lot to put on a Billy Bragg concert. Andy Mac-Donald of the independent Go! Discs, Bragg's label, spent the grand total of £150 on promoting his first LP, *Life's A Riot With Spy Vs Spy*. It subsequently went gold.

Still, it remains true that selling a million copies of an expensively made record is a lot more profitable than selling, say, 50,000 of a cheaply made one. Once you get beyond break-even point, the margin of profit increases dramatically. Betting on the upside pays off – eventually.

Culture Club fall somewhere between the two extremes. There wasn't a lot of hype involved in either the getting of their record contract or the selling of their subsequent records. Someone as charismatic and unusual as George obviates the need for it really. The deal Culture Club got from Virgin was reasonable but not spectacular – by early 1984 they were beginning to resent the amount of money the company were making out of them. They don't take months over making their records and they keep costs to a minimum – often, judging by the complaints I heard in Japan, at the expense of the people who work for them. But like every other pop group, particularly those betting on the upside with a vengeance, in order to get rich they have to spend a lot of time and energy selling their records abroad.

Just under 6 per cent of all the money spent in the world on records and tapes is spent in the United Kingdom. In ascending order, France, the USSR, West Germany, Japan and the USA all account for larger shares of the world market. The USA comprises nearly a third of it. Britain is definitely more of a pop factory than a market. In other words, you don't make the big bucks by staying at home. In fact, most New Pop groups practically flog themselves to death doing precisely the reverse.

A typical year in the life of a group like Culture Club involves visits to the USA, Japan, and most of Europe as well as a lot of work at home. Sometimes they find time to go to Australia or South America too. Sandwiched between all the tours and TV appearances, there are songs to write, LPs to record and, usually, videos to make. Any little spaces that might be left over, both at home and abroad, are filled up with interviews, photo sessions, business meetings and a hundred other little tasks. It's hard work.

In fact, it's not surprising that pop stars crack up occasionally or end up taking altogether too much cocaine to keep themselves on the move.

It seems to be endemic to the situation of the young 1980s entrepreneur – be they Silicon Valley high tech operator, City money-dealer or New Pop star – that they burn themselves out before they're thirty. Anyone older can no longer cope with the frantic push needed to develop a new micro-circuit, the jittery reaction speed necessary to deal with instantaneous electronic financial information from around the world or the pressure of keeping up a relentless schedule of touring, recording and forever living in the public eye. In fact, Culture Club may have already passed the point of no return with their third LP, *Waking Up With The House On Fire*. One of the reasons that was such a duff album was that they'd spent so much time relentlessly promoting their previous product about the globe, they didn't leave themselves enough time for the creative work needed on the new one. Whatever, the carrot of the new capitalism is this: burnt out at thirty the entrepreneur may be, but by that time he or she should have made their pile and be ready to jack it all in.

Very often the problem with pop stars is that by this time they're too addicted to the drug of fame to do the decent thing. Really, a member of Culture Club or Duran Duran need never work another day of their lives. If they're sensible with what they've already earned – which is millions – their investments should take care of them. More, they should enable them to find other creative avenues. Think of George Harrison with his film company or former Monkee, Mickey Dolenz, now a successful TV producer.

Pop groups invest their money in all sorts of things. Property is the most obvious and by far the commonest. They own flats and houses all over the place. A lot of them buy studios. The Who started out looking for rehearsal space and somewhere to store their equipment and ended up owning the entire Shepperton film studio complex. Other groups invest in everything from micro-electronic firms to forestry. Investment is something that pop groups are rather shy about, however. Wasn't pop always supposed to have been *against* capitalism, not a rip-roaring celebration of it? There was, of course, always a degree of hypocrisy to the oppositional stance. The once much-touted

ideology of the 'generation gap' and the artistic pretensions of all 'progressive' music never quite managed to hide the fact that what the groups were *really* doing was making money. Great glittering piles of the stuff.

Although the practitioners of the New Pop are still a lot less guilt-ridden and apologetic about this than their predecessors, there is still some residual shyness. Even when it's blindingly obvious that the reason they're, say, writing their songs in Paris, recording them in the Bahamas and following it all up with a bloody great world tour is because they're having a year out for tax reasons, they will deny this is true until they're blue in the face. Looks like they're deserting their homeland. Or caring more about money than music. Or feeling just a little bit awkward because they've ditched the distinction between art and commerce altogether.

One of the last upholders of the oppositional stance in pop music is Paul Weller, the man who first looked at all the New Pop groups and concluded it was like punk never happened. In early 1985 he penned a rant in the *Melody Maker* against the 'New Pop Aristocracy'.

'Let's name names,' he wrote, and did. 'Wham!, Spandau, the Thompson Twins, Howard Jones, Frankie, Duran Duran, etc., etc. – the positive proof that capitalism doesn't work.'

But relish the idea or not, Weller – like all of the above – is proof that for the pop star capitalism can actually work a treat. Sure, he spends a lot of his time and money working for worthwhile causes, but there's no getting around the fact of his personal wealth. With his profits from the Jam, Weller and his astute manager-father bought the old Polygram Studios at Marble Arch in London and transformed them into their own, profit-spinning Solid Bond Studios.

Weller has always been uneasy walking the tightrope between art and commerce, between his ideals and the money those ideals make for him. Tom Bailey of the Thompson Twins, a group not without ideals of their own, is less embarrassed.

'A multinational corporation,' he says, 'is exactly what we are, in a business sense. We've got a monstrously big turnover internationally. A lot bigger than a lot of companies that are quoted on the Stock Exchange.

'People knock you for admitting that you're into the business side, but every band is. Every successful band is into business. It's an absolute reality. To pretend that you're not, I think, is really irresponsible.'

M E D I A

As day slides into night, the lounge bar of Osaka's Plaza Hotel – or 'Praza' if you're talking to a cab driver – is filled with members of the Culture Club camp engaged in an assortment of subdued revelry. At one table, Bill Button is being gently teased as usual. At another, Helen Terry is sharing a drink and a joke with Phil Pickett and Steve Grainger. Propping up the bar and carrying out some light research into the nature and efficacy of Japanese whisky are press officer Ronnie Gurr and the author of this book.

And way over on the other side of the room, huddled together because no one else will talk to them, are the Fleet Street contingent: Christian Appleyard of the *Sunday People*, who's here officially, John Blake of the *Sun* and Ian Trueman of the *Daily Star*, who aren't. The gossip about Trueman, who nobody's heard of but who's already been christened 'Medallion Man' by the crew, is that he only got the trip because daddy's some higher-up on the paper. He's nervous and embarrassed and clearly a little new to the job.

He has, however, already filed his first story. 'GEORGE

SHOWS OFF HIS JAP LOOK HAIRDO' it's called and bears scant relation to the truth. The nub of it is that George's 'famous locks have been styled to sweep across his face with his chunky plaits dyed white and red – the colours of the Japanese flag.' This is not in fact the case. George's hair is its usual mid-brown, as Trueman would know if he had so much as caught a glimpse of George since arriving in Japan the day before. That he hasn't also casts doubt on the veracity of the two quotes in the story Trueman has attributed to George. 'It's just a simple change. Something new and a little different' and 'It's been a long long journey and I need rest before these concerts.' One is tempted to wander over to his table and express the opinion that if he's going to make up quotes, surely he could have made up some better ones than those. My favourite bit comes at the end of this crisp work of fiction, where an equally banal utterance is said to have sprung from the lips of 'band member Ted Winfield'.

George, Jon, Roy, Mikey . . . *and Ted*?

Ted's actually a roadie and the consensus at the bar is that if Jon Moss were right now to walk into the room, march up to Trueman and announce that not only were his band bigger than Jesus Christ but that they were also giving all their money to the IRA and had just made arrangements to play the first concert on the moon, then Trueman would (*a*) believe him but (*b*) have trouble filing his story because he wouldn't be able to work out just which band it was that Jon was a member of.

Ah, Fleet Street. It's true: you just have to laugh. Otherwise you'd probably want to go and petrol bomb the place.

If we need one word to sum up the relationship between the media and the New Pop, that word is: integration. Pop stars sell newspapers and boost TV ratings. Television appearances and coverage in the daily papers sell records and, of course, make pop stars jolly famous.

The kind of fame the New Pop stars wanted was no longer the youth culture or cult appeal that could be granted by the ailing traditional music press. They wanted to be as famous as

Princess Diana, with whom they're all so fond of comparing themselves. So straight out of the window went anything more than a passing interest in the *NME*, *Melody Maker*, etc. Fleet Street was much more exciting: uncharted territory and read by millions too. Long gone was any nagging remnant of the punk idea that television equalled the Establishment and was therefore detrimental to credibility unless you told Terry Wogan to fuck off or something. Who cared about credibility? The New Pop stars would do anything to get on television. They'd even agree to being locked up in a cage and pelted with custard pies – which was what invariably happened on the now defunct Saturday morning kids' show, *Tiswas* – if that was what it took to get their new video shown. It usually took less than that.

The value of the video boom was something that the practitioners of the New Pop twigged fairly early. Culture Club, it is true, have added little or nothing to the state of this particular art. Their videos have been uniformly awful even by the medium's distinctly dodgy standard. 'I think you're in trouble if your videos are better than your songs,' George has said by way of excuse and this is certainly one of the troubles that Culture Club ran into around the time of *The War Song*. But that was the fault of the songs. Video, meanwhile, has had its promotional possibilities tried, tested and proved true by a score of bands in the wake of Adam, who developed pantomime narratives and introduced guest stars, and Duran Duran, who pioneered the fad for exotic locations and discovered that the easiest way to make a band look interesting was to make them look rich. Many regard video as the secret weapon that won the second British Invasion. The Battle of MTV . . . this was their finest hour.

In 1983, only one British number one single could not boast an accompanying video. *Billboard* has estimated that in 1984 the music industry as a whole shelled out $60 million on over 1500 promotional clips. While these also go to clubs and into video juke boxes – outlets that are only just beginning to be important – their most important use is on television. With MTV, the USA's premier twenty-four-hour, nationwide cable music video channel, the procedure is simple. You make your video and you send it to them. If it fits their criteria (i.e. is by a famous white group or Michael Jackson) then it'll get shown. If it gets shown it'll sell records and encourage radio play. The more attention-grabbing it

is, the more it'll get shown and the more records it'll sell. A couple of years ago, before the American industry caught up in the images race, the New Pop was sweeping all before it on MTV and even the unlikeliest groups – British groups no one had heard of in Britain, the Fixx or A Flock Of Seagulls – were having video-based hits.

With MTV the fact of integration is now as obvious as it has always been with, say, Top Forty radio. In Britain, which has no equivalent of MTV worth mentioning, and where groups regularly arrange to be out of the country just in order to try and get their new clip on *Top Of The Pops* instead of themselves miming, the depth of integration is less obvious. It's reflected instead in the mushroom growth of 'youth related' TV shows that followed the opening of Channel 4 in autumn 1982. Once upon a time, pop music was a rare and valued commodity on British national television. Now it seemed that you could scarcely turn on your set without being confronted by pop stars playing, pop stars talking, pop stars introducing their new videos and pop stars interviewing other pop stars. This was of course nothing compared to MTV, but it was plenty enough for Britain.

Nowhere, however, did the integration of New Pop and media become more complete than it did with the British popular press. In the late 1970s the roost of gossip on Fleet Street was still ruled by the society columnists, fearlessly reporting and wrecking reputations among the rich, famous and aristocratic. In the 1980s, this began to change. Statistically it seems that people tend to remain loyal to whatever paper they started out with. As the circulation war hotted up on Fleet Street, the dailies frantically began trying to catch new readers while they were still in their teens. Enter the era of pop gossip: a new source of scandal, sex, outrage and trivia.

A key figure in this is John Blake. He started the 'Ad Lib' column on the London *Evening News* and moved it to the *Standard* when the papers merged. Then Kelvin McKenzie, an editor whose maxim of 'every page must shock and amaze' seemed to be suited admirably by Blake's style of reporting, lured him to the *Sun*. There, his 'Bizarre' column honed the mixture of trivia and scandal and proved enormously successful. So much so that when Robert Maxwell bought the *Mirror*, he saw Blake's services as essential in his battle to outshine the *Sun*. He offered Blake, oh, any salary he wanted. *Sun* proprietor Rupert Murdoch flew Blake to New York and made him a counter-offer.

'It was ludicrous,' Blake told *Time Out*. 'They were offering me Porsches, jobs in America, you name it. I doubt if either of them had read a word I've written. It was just these two inflated egos bidding for some object they wanted to possess.'

Whatever, Maxwell won. While all the columns Blake launched still carried on much as before, mostly under people who used to work for him, Blake joined the *Mirror* pulling in a salary rumoured to be anything up to £50,000 a year. All around him, Fleet Street was going crazier about pop than it ever had before. It was a fearsome spectacle. Stories about sex and drugs and rock and roll thronged the pages of the dailies, next to stories about the Royal Family and stories about personalities from the soaps and bingo, bingo, bingo. And if the pop stories didn't flood in, why, then the columnists just made them up. Ian Trueman's little 'hairdo' piece from Japan is only a mild example. Blake once invented a story about Culture Club splitting up. And amid all the saucy, soaraway scandal, news hardly got a look in any more.

The New Pop stars, hungry for publicity and thirsting for fame, have for their part been only too happy to co-operate. The *Sun* is, after all, read by an estimated one in every twelve people in Britain. While in music press interviews pop stars would bitch and moan about the treatment they received at the hands of Fleet Street, how the bastards just made it all up, behind the scenes they'd be desperately angling for coverage, often going so far as to make it all up themselves. As Blake told the *NME*:

'Very often you work it out with the artists themselves. The Thompson Twins were desperate to do a series in the *Sun*. I said look, the group are so withdrawn that I don't think I can do anything. So it went backwards and forwards and then they said, all right, we're going to say some amazing things. I sat down with them and Alannah said, "Oh yeah we have affairs intermittently" and said "I'd love to be called – what is it? – the tasteful scarlet lady." We worked it all out. It's all a joke. You work it all out with their co-operation.'

No one was keener to cooperate than Boy George. Emerging with honours from the new romantic school of getting your picture in the papers as often as possible, he launched himself at Fleet Street with an energy and verve that immediately upped the ante enormously.

'Boy George had an attitude. Get a story in the papers every single day,' says Peter Holt, an old Etonian who these days runs the *Standard*'s 'Ad Lib' column. 'He really understood how Fleet Street worked, knew what each paper wanted in a story and how to deliver it. He was brilliant at it. He really set the ball rolling.'

From the moment Culture Club played 'Do You Really Want To Hurt Me' on *Top Of the Pops*, George was never out of the papers. The first stories focussed on his look and was it a boy or was it a girl? Then came George talking about how ordinary he was under all that make-up, believing in love and preferring a good cup of tea to sex and all that. Then came the deluge: George in boxing gloves and George with his mother and George attacking his old headmaster for the way he was treated at school. That last one launched a lengthy debate in the *Times Educational Supplement*. Then there was George saying he was 'just a poof with muscles' and 'admitting' he was bisexual and George falling out with Marilyn and then making friends with him again. There was George with Joan Rivers and how posh London hotel Claridges specially relaxed their 'ties only' rule so he could take tea in her suite. There was George with Robert Mitchum and how Mitchum wanted to adopt him. There was George with Joan Collins – 'The Boy and the Bitch' – which was a Fleet Street double whammy: soap and pop in one story. Next he was linked with royalty. Princess Diana is a fan of George's 'way-out style'. Prince Charles tells a disabled teenager he thinks George is 'quite good'.

It got increasingly ridiculous. Boy George wears wigs shock. An airport security guard claims: 'Boy George swore at me'. Boy George is celibate. Boy George is growing a beard. Boy George has an argument at some party or other and storms out. By this point, if George had so much as tied his shoelaces in public it would have made headlines.

Throughout it all, George played the papers for all they were

worth. Two stories serve to illustrate. In February 1984, George was hanging around a lot with a Japanese journalist called Miko. The papers promptly announced that this was George's 'secret love'. As the pair travelled together for a Culture Club appearance at the San Remo festival, George was stopped by French customs.

'What actually happened was that they let me in,' George told me. 'I got through OK but my friend Miko had left her passport in her bag so I came back to help her. For some reason the woman in the office took a real offence at me and started causing all this fuss. I just said, "You're horrible, go to hell" and wouldn't do anything she told me. She was trying to pull my passport out of my hand and I wouldn't let her have it. And then it turned into a nightmare. We were there for three hours and by the time we got out half the world's press was there. So they did me a favour really.'

What George told the world's press was that French customs wouldn't let him in because they didn't believe the androgynous figure in front of them was the man on his passport photo. 'ALLEZ OOPS! FRENCH GIVE BOY GEORGE LE SEX TEST,' blared the *Sun* the next day, taking the opportunity to give vent to its usual racism and have a dig at the 'hopping mad frogs'. The story went all around the world.

Another story that bounced about the globe was George meeting Princess Margaret at a radio awards ceremony in late May 1984. She was reported afterwards to have asked, 'Who's Boy George, then?' and later referred to him as 'an over made-up tart'. The furore raged in the tabloids for days afterwards, with George demanding a royal apology and Buckingham Palace denying all knowledge of the remark. The joke is, George does seem to have made the whole thing up. He was certainly in a sprightly mood for publicity that day, at another point deliberately using the ladies' loo just so the press could snap him coming out of it. When I arrived in Japan a few weeks later, a cab driver who decided that I must be George went to great lengths in faltering English to tell me he'd read all about this.

But even a master of this manipulative art must eventually fall victim to what those in the PR game term 'the media spiral'. George, like others before him, found the publicity bandwagon running out of control. Photographers followed him everywhere.

From time to time he'd belt one with an umbrella outside a nightclub or swear at a gaggle of paparazzi at Heathrow and that all made the papers too. When he went on holiday to Jamaica, a *Star* photographer camped out on a nearby rooftop the whole time, angling for a shot of George in his swimming trunks. When he got back to England, there was the ruckus outside EMI when he was supposed to have punched a Duran fan. There are those who say the *Sun* set the whole thing up. Whatever, blanket publicity had turned into tiresome overkill. The public were getting bored with George and George was no longer able to keep a firm grip on the level of coverage.

'How can I stop Dave Hogan (a *Sun* photographer) following me down to the supermarket?' he snapped angrily when once I asked him if he didn't think he was overplaying the Fleet Street game.

The thing is, Fleet Street coverage can lead a group to massive success in record time. Wham!, Frankie and Duran Duran have all been helped up to the heights by Fleet Street. Duran Duran even scored on the downward plunge of the spiral. A two-part story in the *Sun* – revenge, apparently for the paper not getting the interview it wanted – dwelt rather spectacularly on their alleged fondness for cocaine. In a curious way, this actually helped the group, lending them a certain grown-up rock and roll credibility.

It also illustrates the fact that pop is big business and the papers need it almost as much as it needs them. When planning his part of a *Mirror* re-launch, John Blake rang Duran's 'controller of publicity', Nick Underwood, to try and arrange a five-part series on the group. Underwood said no. Blake then threatened to send five reporters scurrying anywhere in the world after Duran, keeping the group on constant surveillance. 'We really don't want to do this,' said Blake, 'but we're going to because we need this story.' Underwood still said no. In the end, the *Mirror* cobbled together a piece from interviews with parents and fans. Some weeks later the *Mirror* despatched a reporter to Paris to cover the video shoot for 'A View To A Kill'. Underwood sent him packing. 'But it was interesting,' he says. 'The piece he then wrote was one of the best and most positive Fleet Street have ever written about the group.'

The logic of the media spiral is that Fleet Street will eventually ruin a group as gleefully as it once glorified them. They don't care either way, as long as it all makes good copy. Through a combination of luck and judgement, Duran seem to have got through the difficult stage and are now off the spiral altogether. George's career took a much greater battering when the papers turned against him in autumn 1984. By mid-1985, it was Wham! who were riding at the top of the spiral.

'They are the next most popular thing after the Royal Family,' Wham! publicist Connie Fillipello told *Time Out*. 'I'm trying to stop it. Too much publicity can kill you. But the demand for stories about Andrew and George is so great that the papers just make stories up. It happens every week. Stories about Andrew sleeping with girls he hasn't even met.'

Although it has to be said that in the end, groups get the kind of coverage they ask for. Nobody would make up a story about Boy George sleeping with girls he'd never met. Just as nobody would invent one about Andrew Ridgeley wearing a wig. And before one sheds a tear at the treatment poor Wham! have received, remember that they made up one of the biggest whoppers of them all. Andrew Ridgeley faked a fight, in which he supposedly broke his nose, between himself and his friend David Austin. This was partly to give Austin's recording career some publicity, but mainly to try and cover up the fact that the reason Ridgeley's face was swathed in bandages was because he'd just had a nose job. Wham! even passed that lie on in their own fan club newsletter.

'In the 1970s,' Fillipello went on, 'it was the music press who made acts. Now the music press is a thing of the past. Only *Smash Hits* counts now of the music press.'

As a freelance for that magazine from mid-1981 on, I cannot help but agree with her. Let the circulation figures speak for themselves, however. Just after its launch, in January–June 1979, *Smash Hits* boasted a circulation of 166,200 as against 202,000 for the *NME*, 120,000 for *Sounds*, 149,600 for the *Melody Maker* and 107,700 for *Record Mirror*. By July–December 1984, *Smash Hits* was selling just over half a million, while the circulation of all its original competitors had plummetted: 123,192 for the *NME*, 89,398 for *Sounds*, 71,485 for *Record Mirror* and 68,217 for the *Melody Maker*. *Smash Hits* was by now the ninth biggest-selling magazine in Britain and while a carbon-copy competitor, *Number*

One, had made tremendous strides in circulation since its launch in 1983, overtaking all the other music papers, it was still selling less than half the amount of *Smash Hits*.

But the significance goes deeper than mere figures. *Smash Hits* is a study in another kind of integration. Its rise mirrored exactly the rise of the New Pop; the staples of its coverage were, as each came along, Blondie, Police, Jam, Adam, Spandau, Human League, Duran Duran, Culture Club. With Duran particularly, the relationship was a close one. *Smash Hits* put them on the cover very early in their career and from then on covered every important stage in their career. It boosted both band and magazine as Duran fans everywhere bought every copy. 'You might as well call *Smash Hits* "Duran Hits",' George once muttered sarcastically to me upon being informed that he had once again come second in most categories of a readers' poll.

But of course *Smash Hits* – with its mix of news, reviews, informative and anecdotal features, song lyrics, gossip and quality colour photos – wasn't just about Duran Duran and nor was its integration with the cutting edge of the British music industry confined to its home shores. When British groups began to take off around the world, their fans began to pick up on *Smash Hits* too. Scores of fans I talked to in Japan knew all about it. Likewise in Australia. In January 1984, at the height of the British Invasion, an American cousin, *Star Hits*, began publication under license. The same year a *Smash Hits* was also launched in Australia. With all this and each copy back in Britain selling more than the average number one single, *Smash Hits* turned into a bit of a pop star itself. A fact that was underlined as the *NME*, desparately trying to work out just what had gone wrong in its fall from the prominence of the punk era, name-checked *Smash Hits* several times in each issue. They were usually rather slighting references, rather in the manner the paper looked down from its high horse at, say, Wham!

But what *had* gone wrong with the traditional music press?

Simple really. In the early 1970s, as the music market came to be dominated by the 'thinking fan' and album-buyer, the pop press of the day managed to change with it. The *NME* and *Melody Maker* shifted their coverage from teenagers and the single-buyer to match the needs of the new rock audience. When punk came along, they managed to shift ground to cope with that too. Having gone that far, they found it impossible to pretend that punk had never happened. They could neither switch back to being pop papers – especially futile once *Smash Hits* began mopping up the market – nor find a measured or entertaining perspective on the New Pop. That critics of the *NME* had spent most of 1981 and 1982 attacking the values of rock and questioning the very practice of criticism itself only compounded the problem. By 1983, they were in a mess, floundering around in search of a new constituency without even any idea of how to cling on to the old one, which was dwindling anyway. The New Pop simply didn't make sense in terms of the only criteria the music press could muster up to deal with it, simply didn't look right in artily unfocused monochrome snaps. And there were few people still interested in reading tortured analytical prose about the even fewer remaining groups that did.

While the traditional music press limped off into the sunset of their circulations, *Smash Hits* succeeded by providing everything the New Pop fan could ask for, every fortnight. By reflecting the make-up of the charts and publishing the lyrics of all the hits, it was useful even to the reader without a record player, providing a background to what might be seen on *Top Of The Pops* or heard on Radio 1. If a fan couldn't afford the record, then having the lyrics was the next best thing. Full-page colour pictures on the back, in the centre and elsewhere in the magazine could be removed and stuck in a scrapbook or pinned on a bedroom wall. It was annoying, but a testament to their quality, to see a maverick street trader doing brisk business on Carnaby Street in summer 1984 by selling mounted pages from *Smash Hits* at a quid a throw.

If *Smash Hits* was basically *useful*, it also did its damnedest always to be interesting. Equal attention was paid to everything from the cover feature to the smallest picture caption. It was all given a character. Readers' letters were scrutinized to discover who they wanted to read about and what they wanted to know. If an act had an angle of their own – be that Alison Moyet's chickens or Paul Weller's social conscience – *Smash Hits* would leap on it and sharpen it up. If an act that had to be covered was clearly as boring as a school dinner, we'd rack our brains for some way of brightening them up. At times there was a sense of real joy in making pop stars jump through metaphorical hoops: dressing them up in some absurd outfit or sending them off with a writer and a photographer on some idiotic errand. It was all for their own good, after all. Indeed, some *Smash Hits* features were nothing less than acts of the purest charity, as a writer struggled to gloss over an artist's intellectual failings, hopeless inarticulacy or the fact that they were blind drunk and incoherent throughout the entire interview.

The *Smash Hits* style of journalism is a very benign process. You see what you're allowed to see and write about what you see. No digging for dirt and only a little challenging of motives, but a constant gentle piss-taking of everything and everybody. At times it's enormous fun: travelling, if you're lucky, to exotic faraway climes and meeting interesting people, vicariously fulfilling at least some of the wishes of a million fans. At other times it's curiously depressing, sitting in a pokey room in a record company's offices, listening to some one-hit wonder who you know is going to be chewed up and spat out by the pop machine in a matter of weeks, mouthing off at great length about their drab hopes and fears.

Before I got involved in the music industry, I considered it to be totally venal and corrupt. It therefore surprised me that I liked so many of the people I began to meet. A fair majority of the pop stars I've come across have been charming and interesting people, if usually a little self-obsessed. Few, though, match up to their manufactured mystique. A star like George, who does, is rare indeed. You tend to develop curious, stunted relationships with the people you interview more than once. However well you get on, however close you manage to become, they can never quite trust you and you can never quite be sure of them. Pop stars in any case move in a different dimension from we ordinary mortals. The first time you meet them they've very likely just hit the limelight, are thrilled by all the attention and are often slightly in awe of a journalist they've heard of. You feel protective, almost fatherly. If they don't disappear straight down the dumper, all too often the next time you bump into them they've turned into horrid, snotty, self-important nouveau millionaires and are off-hand and unnecessarily rude. You then feel like smacking them.

Deep down, most pop stars harbour a quiet contempt for even the most sympathetic of journalists. If you honestly express an adverse opinion about some aspect of their work – never mind gratuitously slagging them off – they hate and revile you and never talk to you again. If you're nice about them, then they almost invariably start taking advantage of you.

But that, of course, is what the relationship between the New Pop and the media is all about.

12
LIKE PUNK NEVER HAPPENED

I
n January 1985, an American friend of mine, resident in London, told me he'd met a young hairdresser from some hick town in Ohio. She was over here to learn some of the new tricks of her trade: artificial hair extensions and so forth. My friend is from New York and knows no more about life in Hicktown, Ohio, than I do, so he asked her about it. Did she like living there? Oh yes. What did Hicktonians do for fun in the evenings? Well, they watched TV and went to the movies and listened to music and . . . you know, all sorts of things. What kind of music did they like?

'Oh, we have Boy George,' she replied. Everyone in Hicktown knew Boy George. 'But no one really likes him any more since he had his hair cut.'

At first I assumed this was simply the opinion of a hairdresser – a hairdresser who, after all, was learning a technique that George and Roy Hay had done a lot to popularize. If it weren't for Culture Club, why else would there be a demand for hair extensions in Hicktown, Ohio? But over the next few months, as I quizzed friends and colleagues who returned from the States, I heard the same thing over and over again. Whether it was in Louisiana or Los Angeles, what was being said seemed to boil down to the same simple equation:

George minus locks equals turkey.

Once upon a time it was accepted music business wisdom that (*a*) it took bloody ages to crack the American market but that (*b*) once you had, you could rely on doing business there for long after the fickle British pop public had thrown you over for some Next Big Thing. No longer. Culture Club had already watched America fall at the merest flutter of George's eyelashes. In the winter of 1984–5, they also began to learn that the new American pop market they'd helped to create could be just as capricious and inconstant as any other. Not that America was the only place where they were beginning to fall from grace.

'We don't believe in disturbing a successful formula.' In Japan I got really bored with hearing people say that. It was like a Culture Club motto, to be trotted out whenever there was any discussion of their future plans. Were they still working with producer Steve Levine on the new LP? 'Yes, we don't believe in disturbing a successful formula.' When would the new LP be coming out? 'In the first week of October, the same time of year we released our first two LPs. You see, we don't believe in disturbing a successful formula.' On and on.

At that point there was no doubting that their formula *was* successful. There they were, taking Japan by storm, with God only knows how many record sales behind them and George a celebrity everywhere from the slopes of Mount Fuji to the hairdressing salons of Hicktown, Ohio. After Japan, they'd be jetting off for their first tour of Australia. There, scenes of hitherto unimagined hysteria would unfold. They would be mobbed everywhere, close on a thousand fans would gather outside wherever they were staying and in Adelaide – a city of under a million people they would only visit for an afternoon having been unable to find any venue large enough to play – literally scores of thousands of people would turn out just to see them receiving the keys of the city.

Yes, it's a successful formula. Don't disturb it.

But there – right there – lies the seed of Culture Club's mistake number one. Over-confidence. The formula is successful. We're doing everything right. As long as we stick to the formula our future is secure. You could sense it in Jon's offhand attitude to their lack of rehearsal for the tour. All the backing musicians were really worried but Jon didn't care. It'll be all right. We've played this set so many times before. We know the formula and the formula is successful. George could go out there and blow his nose and the fans would still scream and swoon and go away happy. At the time, this was undoubtedly true, but it still made me uneasy to see them taking so much for granted.

Then there were the arguments. However much George might pass them off as meaningless family tiffs – which is definitely what most of them were – it was clear in Japan that there were real rifts developing in the group. Mikey, for instance, felt right out on a limb. There's Roy doing all the arrangements and working closely with George on the songs as well as playing guitar and keyboards. There's Jon keeping an eye on business and mixing all the recordings as well as being the drummer. There's George being George. What does Mikey do? He's just the bass-player. On tour it's even worse. George and Jon stick together. Mikey used to stick with Roy but now Alison's with him all the time. So Mikey feels left out, lonely, powerless and ultimately resentful. Why should he put himself out for 'George's group'? His reluctance to cooperate makes George angry with him and this just makes Mikey even more huffy. Back in Britain it got even worse with Mikey failing to turn up for things like the main *Waking Up With The House On Fire* photo session. Publicity pictures were released without him in them.

On the video shoot for 'The War Song', George complained that he just couldn't understand what Mikey was up to. 'He's just not cooperating as far as I can make out. You can't keep carrying someone around on a stretcher twenty-four hours a day. I put everything I've got into this band and if someone's not pulling their weight then it's just really depressing. No, it won't come to throwing him out. I haven't got that power anyway.'

173

But they did later come to an agreement with Mikey that if he didn't turn up to songwriting sessions, then he couldn't expect any royalties from the compositions of the others. This was a significant departure from the group's normal practice of splitting everything four ways, no matter who'd contributed what. Mikey's getting on fine with the others these days, but while all the arguments were being broadcast in the press, it didn't do the group's public image much good.

It hadn't been doing their songs much good either. Jon: 'We booked two or three weeks to do the songwriting (for *Waking Up With The House On Fire*) and didn't use one day of it. We had an argument and we left. We tried again three days later and had another argument. We rowed and rowed and George smashed his tape recorder and I threw a chair at him. Then we wrote the album in four days.'

Which almost certainly wasn't long enough. In complete contrast to *Colour By Number*, the songs on *Waking Up* were boring, ill-conceived, unmelodic and badly-constructed. The lyrics were pretty duff too. Perhaps running out of things to pastiche in their policy of making every song different, they ditched the soul and reggae they'd hitherto adapted so brilliantly and opted instead for a half-assed muddle of rock and American MOR. The one track that really worked was 'Mistake Number Three', a poignant ballad about fans growing up. Most of the rest should have been either radically reworked or thrown in the bin, but if the group realized this, they were keeping quiet.

'It's got great music and great melodies as well,' Roy told me while they were still working on it. 'To be quite honest, I know it's a big-headed thing to say, but I love it.'

Apart from being an example of their over-confidence, this also highlights one of the problems of complete control. If the record company had been able to, they should have told the group the LP was awful and made them go back into the studio to smarten it up. But leaving their successful formula undisturbed, they bunged it out, as usual, in early October. Thereafter it cranked up only a tiny fraction of the sales that had been achieved by *Colour By Numbers* – although that was admittedly a hard act to follow.

While too big to be bossed about, George had also been too

busy being a star to find anything but the circumstances of his fame to write songs about. It's a classic trap and he fell into it head first. 'Being a pop star is like being thrown out of a window naked, hence the title,' is how he explained the album, on which one song was sarcastically dedicated to 'John Blake and your big value *Sun*' and another to Alison English, the girl who claimed he'd punched her on the nose. 'Everyone wants to scrutinize you, see you naked. You become property. Hot property. The sleeve symbolizes persecution.'

I mean, who cares? As George himself said later in the same interview: 'Anybody who starts a career in music is a first-class show-off and if you turn around six months later and say you don't like it, you're a liar.' And why should anyone looking to pop music for a lift and a laugh and a shot of good old-fashioned glamour want to hear about how terrible it is being a world-famous multi-millionaire? In fact, having seen him in the papers just about every day for the last two years, people were bored enough with George without him adding to the irritation by bemoaning the intrusiveness of all the publicity he'd quite clearly set in motion himself.

Then there was the competition. By now Wham! had moved into the centre of the pop stage, writing simpler, more effective pop songs than Culture Club and watching them shoot to the top of charts all over the place. Early in the year, with a spate of paralysing legal problems behind them, they announced that they'd have four British number ones before 1984 was out. With 'Wake Me Up Before You Go Go', 'Careless Whisper' and 'Freedom', they managed three. Their fourth single, 'Last Christmas', only failed to make the top spot because Band Aid's 'Do They Know It's Christmas?' – in which Wham!, along with just about every other British pop group, were involved – was holding off against all comers. Culture Club's 'The Medal Song', meanwhile didn't even make the top thirty.

George's sensationalism was also taking a battering from all directions. The clone wars between him, Marilyn and Pete Burns of Dead Or Alive – with all three bitching constantly about each other in the press – raged for the first half of 1984. George seemed to win, but only by adopting a lofty moral tone that led many to christen him the Pope of Pop. A lot of his thunder was stolen in the process. What little remained of George's shock value was undermined by the arrival of Frankie Goes To Hollywood, with banned records, banned videos, two of the biggest-selling British singles ever (both 'Relax' and 'Two Tribes' outdid 'Karma Chameleon') and an awful lot of fuss about sex, gay politics and nuclear war. They and George had the odd skirmish in private. There was some incident in a studio involving fire extinguishers and a lot of obscenities being shouted down a phone – Frankie are notorious pranksters. George then moaned about it in public and simply made himself look stupid.

'The only people interested in Culture Club now are middle-aged women. He's not upsetting anyone. He's not breaking down any barriers,' said Frankie's in-house clone, Paul Rutherford, in *Jamming!* magazine, turning George's usual argument right back at him.

'He's just establishment. The only reason he gets away with it is because he sings nice little songs. I don't think he's at all interested in breaking down any barriers. He just does it for himself. He knows who's buttering his fucking bread now. That's why he's been going on about Princess Diana being the best-dressed woman in Britain. He's turned into something of a monster. To everyone, he's just a singer. If you stuck on a porn movie with two fellas . . . it would be just the same as it's always been. You can only get away with it if you look like Boy George. It doesn't mean that you can walk around with a pair of leather knickers on. Boy George, at the very most, is like an English eccentric. He sounds like Matt Monro or something.'

All this was taking its toll on George. Always torn between trying to be the lovable Boy next door and deep down wanting really to be the most outrageous person on the planet, the delicate balance he'd been maintaining with Jon's help began to tip. A vengeful Georgina was on the rise. Much to the group's dismay, she began appearing in public with rubber-clad transvestites, talking to magazines like *Woman's Own* about the Royal Family having 'their fair share of thieves like everyone else' and running through a frantic series of wigs and image changes in a last ditch attempt to recapture some of the old outrage.

The only result was to confuse people. When the natives of Hicktown, Ohio, complain about George cutting his hair off, what they really resent is his departure from the whole dreadlocks and

Hasidic hat look that they'd found so safe and cosy and learnt to love. It was a gradual transition, but by May 1985 George was appearing in a *Smash Hits* centrespread wearing a suit and a tie and staring sternly at the camera from beside a collage of rippling naked male torsos. For the first time, he was actually presenting a sexually threatening figure.

In October 1984, Culture Club embarked on their second US tour of the year. Whereas the first had begun with some 3000 fans cheering their arrival at Montreal airport, this one started with them only filling 15,000 of the 19,000 seats at a Dallas venue and with hundreds of protesters outside every night bearing banners that proclaimed, 'Boy George Is Evil' and 'If Sex Is A Sin, What Is Boy George?'. Back in Britain, the press pounced. George's honeymoon with Fleet Street was long over and headlines began loudly declaring the tour a total flop. The American media also launched into a baying backlash. In reality, things weren't really as black as they were being painted. Culture Club were after all taking their show for the first time to some of the most conservative parts of America. And after Dallas, they had no problem selling out most of the rest of the dates. Still, having boasted overconfidently in Japan that they could sell out Madison Square Garden five nights in a row and fill the 80,000 capacity Anaheim stadium twice over, they managed only one night at the Garden and didn't play Anaheim at all.

'The War Song' was only a minor American hit, 'Mistake Number Three' barely dented the top fifty and *Waking Up With The House On Fire* hung around the album charts for a while but could hardly be declared a triumph. By Spring 1985, everyone from the American media to the hairdressers of Hicktown, Ohio, were apparently united in the opinion that Culture Club were so far down the dumper they'd never be able to clamber out again.

Boy George is also coming in for some stick several thousand miles away in the distinctly tacky, red plush and oak panel surrounds of the Quasimodo Club, San Remo, Italy. That is to say, as pop star after pop star, all in this normally sleepy retirement town for the annual 'playback' festival, file into the club, Nash and Mark of Frankie Goes To Hollywood are doing their usual camp impersonation of 'Larry Lamb', as they call him. Singing along to 'The War Song' in ridiculous, high-pitched voices, they pat the air in unison to left and right, smiling inanely.

Elsewhere in the club or in the queue, are the rest of Frankie, Spandau Ballet, Duran Duran, Sade and the Village People. Elsewhere in town are Chaka Khan, Bronski Beat, Jermaine Jackson and a host of lesser pop stars. Culture Club are, in fact, notable by their absence. Last year they were topping the bill. But it's probably just as well they're not here. Frankie – this year's headliners – can't stand George. And if Frankie can't stand someone, chances are they'll do something about it, their current prank of dropping a Yohji Yamamoto carrier bag full of water on his head, maybe. And with that he'd be getting off lightly.

Nash, completely 'bladdered' already, is staggering about, pointing at people and announcing: '*You* are scum. *You* are shite.' Mark O'Toole has just bought a young lady a drink and is gently sliding his arm along the back of the sofa, moving in for the kill, when Nash reels up to ruin his chances. 'If you don't have her fuckin' kit off in thirty seconds,' he shouts, 'then *you* are a poof and *you* are a shite!'

In one corner, Nick Rhodes of Duran and Paul Rutherford of Frankie are having a nice little chat about Art. In another, Frankie's Holly Johnson is engaged in heated debate with the Village People. Close by where Duran's John Taylor is propped precariously against the bar, Spandau's Gary Kemp – clad, like everyone else, in an outfit that probably cost enough to feed a family of four for six months – is bending the ear of *Smash Hits* editor Mark Ellen about the miners' strike, being working class and all that. Nearby, his brother Martin, biting back his envy of Paul Rutherford's Yamamoto cloak, is pulling pearls from his necklace and throwing them at people. Nick Rhodes grabs someone's camera and flits about, snapping everyone. 'Don't bother with that, Nick,' taunts Spandau drummer John Keeble. 'They're bound to be crap, just like your book!'

The New Pop aristocracy at play. To say it's like punk never happened is like saying Nash – at this precise moment busy dancing on a table with Duran's Andy Taylor to the tune of Sam the Sham's 'Woolly Bully' – enjoys the occasional drink.

As Simon le Bon chats to a TV pop show hostess and Steve Norman tells Mark O'Toole how Spandau are 'outselling Springsteen in Australia', Andy Taylor is buzzing around telling everyone that they're all 'poufs' and 'wankers'. Nasher, he declares in a challenging tone, has very probably only got a small 'chopper'. Nash hotly denies this slur on his manhood. It is Andy, who is scum and a shite, that is clearly deficient in this department. And so the fag-end of the evening finds the pair of them lowering their trousers and comparing the dimensions of their respective organs.

The winner was not announced.

T he wheel just turned again. Did you notice? The New Pop might never have been able to lay claim to any *perfect moment*, none of the people involved might ever had made much fuss about being 'from the streets' or anything punky like that, but by early 1985 they were further from their audiences than ever before, whirled off into a star system which their fans could only gaze up at wonderingly from afar.

Replacing café society as the prime material of the gossip columns, the same few faces stared out from the daily papers every morning, chumming around in clubs or at parties. Draped in silks, dripping with pearls and clothed in extravagant and expensive outfits from the same litany of fashionable designers – Yohji Yamamoto, Jean-Paul Gaultier, Issey Miyake, Gianni Versace – they even looked more aristocratic than the upper crust of Hooray Henries and simpering Sloanes whose places they'd taken. Even George, who'd always carefully crafted an image that fans could copy, had suddenly transformed himself into a designer-clad luxury item.

Abroad most of the time, in foreign studios, on tour or in tax exile, they returned to Britain only to appear on television or play concerts in a handful of the biggest and therefore most impersonal venues. At some point in their careers, while the memory of punk still glowed dimly, all of these bands had declared they'd never play Wembley Arena. By January 1985, they'd not only all played there, but were damn proud of it too. The run up to Christmas 1984 was like a competition. Who could sell out the most consecutive nights there? Duran had set the record with five in 1983. Now Culture Club and Spandau both topped that with six. Hot on their heels came Wham! with four. The Thompson Twins managed three. Paul Young came in last with two. Indeed, with Band Aid topping the charts, Wham! at number two and not one but two Duran Duran specials on national TV, the whole of the Christmas period seemed to have become one long grand celebration of the New Pop.

Or one long last gasp.

Band Aid, in a sense, had a lot to answer for. Towards the end of November 1984, Duran Duran, Culture Club and Spandau Ballet had all jetted back to Britain to join a host of other pop stars and about half a dozen film crews in the making of 'Do They Know It's Christmas?'. Although nothing but laudable in terms of the huge amounts of money the project raised for victims of the famine in Ethiopia, it was also seen as a public celebration of the power of British pop music. They were all 'establishment' now, no doubt about that. And there they all were, patting each other on the back in an orgy of self-congratulation. All, that is, except Paul Weller. He'd carped so long and loud about all these 'Tory groups' that none of them would talk to him.

From that point on, groups were never as bitchy about each other as they'd been in the halcyon days of 1983. With the exception of George, who kept his distance, they were suddenly like one big gang, bumping into each other in various locations about the globe, having a drink and a laugh. San Remo was a classic example. Spandau and Duran appearing together on the British TV show *Pop Quiz* just before Christmas was another. They fought it out amiably (Duran won) and then disappeared off for a drink. By contrast, months previously Culture Club, Duran and

Police had all appeared on the same edition of *Saturday Superstore*. The Police refused to appear in the same shot as either of the other groups. And when Duran and Culture Club all sat round together reviewing videos after a year spent slagging each other off in every corner of the globe, the air fair crackled with tension.

The result of all this public chumminess was a distinct deadening of the whole phenomenon. Over the past few years, their fans had been gathering like tribes, drawing strength from the attentions and successes of the groups they followed, taking their battles to heart. What did they do now, faced by a grinning, champagne-swilling united front of the New Pop aristocracy? It suddenly meant less to express an undying preference for, say, Spandau Ballet over Duran Duran when there for all to see were Gary Kemp and John Taylor sharing a drink and a joke without a trace of competition or animosity.

Competition had always been the life-blood of the New Pop when the groups were on the way up. It was exciting. Who would beat who to number one? Who was going to crack America first? Who could slag off the greatest number of rival pop stars in one brief *Smash Hits* interview? Now they were all on top, rolling in the fruits of massive international success and all they wanted was to stay there. The only question left was: who could last ten years up there? The only remaining bone of contention – it had come to this – was who would be the new Queen?

The New Pop was congealing, going stale. While sheer momentum was filling Wembley Arena God knows how many times over, the British charts were beginning to tell a different story. Boring AOR – adult-oriented rock – like Sade and Alison Moyet was outselling just about everything else in the album charts. The singles charts were in the throes of an American counter-invasion: Madonna, Prince, Bruce Springsteen, ZZ Top, Bryan Adams, 'We Are The World'. Colourless characters like Nik Kershaw and Howard Jones used the routes the New Pop had mapped out to purvey a dull, dated rock mish-mash. Groups like King and Dead Or Alive, who by rights should never have been anything more than mere footnotes to pop history, started having big hit singles.

In spring 1985, one looked around and wondered what had happened to it all. Spandau Ballet were squabbling with their record company. Culture Club had retired to lick their wounds and plan a comeback. The Thompson Twins, after one not terribly successful single, were out of action because singer Tom Bailey had collapsed. Duran Duran were racked with internal tensions and preoccupied with a rash of side projects. Paul Young had turned into another grown-up AOR act. Wham! were off in foreign parts and, if rumours were to be believed, in danger of splitting up. Frankie, having got three British number ones with their first three singles, turned into another boring rock group and disappeared into tax exile. In fact most of them were in tax exile. There were more British pop stars in Paris than there were in London. Nick Rhodes would take a break from recording there with Simon le Bon to go out to dinner with fellow Parisian Roy Hay. Dave Stewart of the Eurythmics bought a flat there. George and Marilyn would pop over to a party at Regine's. Gary Kemp would bump into Frankie on the Champs Elysées and chirp, without a trace of surprise: 'How's it going, lads? Any good clubs about?'

Yes indeed, the wheel had turned.

Wham! were now the new sensation wowing everyone from Hicktown, Ohio, to the slopes of Mount Fuji and beyond, even to the pop-starved citizenry of communist China. But as Wham! took the lead it signalled a subtle change. Gone, with them, were the last vestiges of New Romantic flash and idealism. Scratch the surface of any of the original New Pop groups and you'd find something, however slight, underneath. Spandau Ballet saw their work as art and underpinned it with an ideology of working-class aspiration. Duran Duran did their best to explore what could be done with a pop video, tried to avoid settling into the obvious with their singles, and with 'The Reflex', 'The Wild Boys' and 'A View To A Kill', it began to pay off. Culture Club issued a comprehensive challenge to sexual stereotyping and asked questions about the 'politics of living'.

But Wham! aimed to be nothing more than they seemed to be: two nice middle-class boys busy making a fortune. After their first couple of singles, their songs didn't even seem to spring from their own experiences. It was all just George Michael playing with imaginary emotions and situations. Scratch the suburban surface of Wham! and you'd find nothing beneath but nagging disillusion.

Frankie Goes To Hollywood illustrated a change of a different kind. Having kicked around for a year or two, trying to get noticed by being as outrageous as possible but failing to raise anything more than a passing interest from all the major labels, they were finally offered a deal by ZTT. It wasn't much of a deal – £250 advance and a five per cent royalty – but they took it anyway. Once signed, they were denied even a semblance of control. Their music was taken in hand by Trevor Horn, who extracted the odd bits he liked and spent months putting together the rest by himself. Just about everything else – videos, record sleeves, T-shirts, adverts, books, sleeve notes and all the other things the New Pop had fought so long and hard to control – were master-minded by budding McLaren and former *NME* journalist Paul Morley.

It was all, of course, ludicrously successful – the biggest splash since the Sex Pistols and all that – but that's not the point. The wheel had now turned full circle. The record company called all the shots, took a fair share of the limelight, a more than fair share of the profits and was once more in complete control.

It was like punk had never happened.

POSTSCRIPT

I wrote most of this book in a cold and cheerless office, rented for the duration, just round the corner from the Carburton Street squat where George and his cronies once bitched and bedded down and battled over hairspray. It took me the first few months of 1985. As I began, George was holidaying in the Jamaican sun with Jon, who rapidly fled the island, and Marilyn, who stuck around. George then went to New York City to work on the manuscript of his autobiography, *A Parade Of Assumptions*. While I huddled close to a faltering electric fire and gloomily pondered strategies for unblocking the forever clogged-up office sink, George was ensconced in the doubtless more congenial surrounds of the penthouse suite of Morgan's Hotel on Madison Avenue. Not, from the reports and rumours that filtered back, that it sounded like he was getting much work done.

In his first real break from the group since they sailed to international stardom and without a watchful Jon or Tony Gordon to keep a check on his wilder side, George let himself go completely. He'd be seen around Manhattan, blowing a small fortune with a joyfully reckless abandon and disporting himself in a manner that made his past puritanical pronouncements about drugs, drink and casual sex seem – though I've no doubt he meant them all at the time – like the purest hypocrisy. George, went the joke around Virgin records, was turning into a rock monster. So much had his appearance deteriorated under this new, debilitating regimen, that when he arrived back in London in mid-March, he passed by the *paparazzi* at Heathrow airport with a bag over his head. Even after he'd had a week in bed, his pallor was still sufficient to shock those who saw him around during the London Fashion Week parties.

By the time I was finishing this manuscript, the office was a bit warmer, the sink was still blocked and George was in Europe. Neither Jon nor Tony Gordon, it seemed, had succeeded in calming him down and rumours of genuinely outrageous behaviour at the Paris fashion shows flashed back across the Channel. The group began recording their fourth album in Montreux, Switzerland, with Arif Mardin taking over production from Steve Levine. While waiting to do his vocals, always one of the last stages in the recording process, George – more or less out of harm's way in a quiet house by a lake – continued work on his book.

In July 1985, I found myself at Live-Aid in Philadelphia. While actor Jeff Bridges gushed 'the seeds of Woodstock growing up stronger and more beautiful' and Duran Duran followed the re-formed Crosby, Stills, Nash and Young on to the stage, something suddenly struck me. With the host of artists appearing, from Paul McCartney to Madonna, the event was tantamount to a history of rock since the Beatles – with one omission. Punk. Only Bob Geldof and the Boomtown Rats, who were never authentically punk anyway, stood as a reminder that punk had happened.

Actually, there was another omission. Culture Club. After a lot of humming and hahing about whether or not they could appear, the group had finally decided that they would. And then their management went and forgot to ring up Bob Geldof before the deadline. Culture Club did however play a concert in Athens later that month and were literally stoned by the audience. It seemed they'd hit rock bottom.

But George, interviewed around this time by *Smash Hits*, was philosophical about it all. He admitted their third album was 'rubbishy', that he'd been keeping out of the public eye as much as possible and for once spoke frankly about his homosexuality. He referred to the winter of 1984–5 as his 'self-destructive phase' and seemed well back on form.

In the middle of what was a particularly bad summer for pop music, it was nice to have him back.

One of the many things that working at *Smash Hits* taught me was never, ever to write anyone off. No sooner would a group be judged to have disappeared down the dumper than they'd come triumphantly bouncing back with a top ten single. Every press photograph, no matter how obscure the subject, was dutifully kept and filed away. You never know. Even the dullest-looking member of some miserably contrived group who arrive from nowhere to have one wretched single bought briefly into the top fifty before disappearing once more into decent obscurity might later turn into a sensation that sets charts ablaze and fans a-quiver all over the globe.

The gods of pop are fickle.

So, despite the marked dip in Culture Club's popularity that followed the release of *Waking Up With The House On Fire*, it's clear that they could suddenly soar right back up to the heights. After all, every group has a flop once in a while. Their decision to draw Phil Pickett, co-writer of 'Karma Chameleon' and 'It's A Miracle', back into the writing process, to lure Helen Terry back to do backing vocal arrangements and to have the excellent Arif Mardin at the controls only makes their return more plausible.

On the other hand, nothing is certain until the album is released sometime in early 1986. If George continues to flout his darker side in public and strays ever further from the lovable, down-to-earth character who first conquered the hearts of the world, then even a batch of extraordinarily good songs might not be sufficient to stem the slide down the slippery slope to oblivion. With Culture Club, as with every true pop phenomenon, the excitement and aura of sudden and massive success is at least as important as the product being sold. When you've been that big, that rapidly, then even a couple of steps back down the ladder looks, from the vantage-point of a neck-craning public, like an ignominious belly-flop into the depths. Momentum is all. Lose too much and people lose interest. There are plenty of other hungry attention-seekers to rush in and take your place.

And even if the next album is a success, and the next one, and the one after that, there will come a point where Culture Club will have to go their separate ways. George, who has always felt nothing in common with Roy and Mikey, will likely be the one to depart. Once the group ceases effectively to fuel his fame, he'll up and off and go it alone.

And what then?

We can hazard the odd guess.

Roy will carry on frittering away his fortune on expensive clothes, cars and Cartier jewellery for Alison. He'll do the music for a minor film or two and compose the theme tune for a Channel 4 chat show. In his studio at home, he'll make a dull solo LP or two, painstakingly multi-tracking all the instruments himself. Neither will sell very well and eventually he'll give up the ghost and move to Marbella, living off the chain of laundrettes in Essex that was his only ever sensible investment.

Mikey will move to Los Angeles, do a bit of freelance bass-playing and song-writing and become a Hollywood socialite. He'll be seen from time to time, arriving at an art opening or a film premiere with yet another blonde model on his arm. Well-respected in musicianly circles, he'll live a lazy life and enjoy every minute of it.

Jon will stay in England. After a couple of minor successes, he'll give up trying to be a record producer and will move to the country and become a gentleman farmer. While hired hands shovel the shit, he'll try and write a novel but will never get it finished. He'll lose a lot of his money investing in a dodgy micro-electronics company, but it won't matter. His natural parsimony and his family fortune will see him through to a dignified old age.

And George?

For a while, he'll just live off the chat show circuit but eventually will get some kind of cabaret act together. He'll talk and sing and make set-piece jokes and appear in Las Vegas and Sun City. For a time he'll be like a superior Liberace, but gradually his popularity will slide and people will lose interest as he finds it ever more difficult to mask his advancing years with hair dye and make-up.

When his fortune has all but run out, he'll invest the last bit of it in a wine bar on the Old Kent Road. He'll call it Queenie's and the walls will be covered with platinum discs and Culture Club memorabilia. Helen Terry will be found there most nights, the local lush. Marilyn and Philip Sallon will pop in from time to time to see the drag show on Thursday nights. On quiet evenings, George will entertain the clientele with stories of his past triumphs. Those too young to remember them will now and again stare idly at the yellowing newspaper clippings over the bar. They'll shake their heads at the preposterous clothes people used to wear back in the 1980s, cock half an ear at George rambling on about the good old days and wonder just what was supposed to have been so special about it all.

SOURCES

My principal source for this book has been my own experiences and interviews. I've referred constantly to back copies of *Smash Hits* and *The Face* and have also looked occasionally at odd pieces from *Time Out*, *Blitz*, *Jamming!*, *Rolling Stone* and even the *NME*. The following books have also proved useful:

Ian Birch (ed.), *The Book With No Name*, Omnibus, 1981

Julie Burchill and Tony Parsons, *The Boy Looked At Johnny*, Pluto Press, 1978

Ian Buruma, *A Japanese Mirror*, Jonathan Cape, 1984

Robert C. Christopher, *The Japanese Mind*, Pan, 1984

Al Clark (ed.), *The Rock Yearbook 1982*, Virgin Books, 1981

Quentin Crisp, *The Naked Civil Servant*, Flamingo, 1983

Kasper De Graaf and Malcolm Garrett: *When Cameras Go Crazy*, Virgin Books, 1983

Simon Frith, *Sound Effects*, Constable, 1983

Dick Hebdige, *Subculture: The Meaning Of Style*, Methuen, 1979

Allan Jones (ed.), *The Rock Yearbook Volume V*, Virgin Books, 1984

John Lahr, *Automatic Vaudeville*, Heinemann, 1984

Jim Miller (ed.), *The Rolling Stone Illustrated History Of Rock 'n' Roll*, Picador, 1981

Simon Napier-Bell, *You Don't Have To Say You Love Me*, Nomis Books, 1983

Tim Rice, Jo Rice, Paul Gambaccini and Mike Read, *The Guinness Book Of British Hit Singles*, Guinness Superlatives, 1983

Sue Steward and Sheryl Garratt, *Signed, Sealed And Delivered*, Pluto Press, 1984

Neil Tennant (ed.), *The Best Of Smash Hits*, EMAP Books, 1985

Michael Wale, *Voxpop*, Harrap, 1972

Charles White, *Little Richard*, Pan, 1985

Smash Hits Yearbooks 1983, 1984 and *1985*, EMAP National Publications

ACKNOWLEDGEMENTS

First and foremost, special thanks to Neil Tennant, my agent, editor and collaborator on this book, without whom it would never have got written.

Special thanks also to Ian Birch and Kasper De Graaf for reading the manuscript and for a lot of interesting and useful conversations over the last few years.

Many thanks also to the following for help, advice, support, inspiration, encouragement and information: Terri Anderson, Lisa Anthony, Simon Booth, David 'Scoffer' Bostock, Barbara Charone, The Chelsea Club, André Csillag, Tracy Drew, Petra Elkan, Mark Ellen, Robert Elms, Sheryl Garratt, Malcolm Garrett, Peter Gerard-Pearse, Ronnie Gurr, Tom Hibbert, Kim Hickey, Carolyn Jennings, David Keeps, Jane Lowes, Don Macpherson, Peter Martin, John Maybury, Hilary Potter, Suzie Rome, Helen Terry, Adam Sanderson, Jon Savage, Nick Underwood, Eric Watson and Lesley White.

And last but not least, thanks to anyone and everyone who worked in and around *Smash Hits* over the last few years.

Dave Rimmer

Printed in Great Britain
by Amazon.co.uk, Ltd.,
Marston Gate.